This Land Is OUR LAND

A HISTORY OF AMERICAN IMMIGRATION

★ ★ ★ ★ ★ ★ ★ ★ ★ ★ ★ ★ ★

LINDA BARRETT OSBORNE

★ ★ ★ ★ ★ ★ ★ ★ ★ ★ ★ ★ ★

ABRAMS BOOKS FOR YOUNG READERS • NEW YORK

In memory of my great-grandparents—
the Boccuzzis, Valeris, Marinos, and Cerones—
and for immigrants who continue to come to our
country with courage and hope

Library of Congress Cataloging-in-Publication Data

Osborne, Linda Barrett, 1949–
This land is our land : the history of American immigration /
by Linda Barrett Osborne.
pages cm
Includes bibliographical references and index.
ISBN 978-1-4197-1660-7 (alk. paper)
1. United States—Emigration and immigration—History—Juvenile
literature. 2. Immigrants—United States—History—Juvenile
literature. I. Title.
E184.A1O83 2016
304.80973—dc23
2015017877

Text copyright © 2016 Linda Barrett Osborne
Book design by Maria T. Middleton & Sara Corbett
For illustration credits, see page 121.

Printed and bound in China

10 9 8 7 6 5 4 3 2

Abrams Books for Young Readers are available at special
discounts when purchased in quantity for premiums and
promotions as well as fundraising or educational use. Special
editions can also be created to specification. For details, contact
specialsales@abramsbooks.com or the address below.

ABRAMS The Art of Books
115 West 18th Street, New York, NY 10011
abramsbooks.com

CONTENTS

INTRODUCTION

All eight of my great-grandparents were born in Italy.

They came to the United States in the 1880s and 1890s. At least two of them arrived before 1892, when Ellis Island opened to process the millions of people emigrating from Europe. My great-grandparents were immigrants to this country.

So were the English settlers of Jamestown, Virginia, in 1607, and the Pilgrims, in 1620.

The United States is a nation of immigrants and their descendants. The ancestors of everyone who lives here, except for the Native Americans "discovered" in North America by Europeans in the early sixteenth century, came from somewhere else. (The slaves brought from Africa also came from across the Atlantic, although they came against their will. Theirs is a separate story.) Most Americans—even those who call for limits on immigration—have an image of our country as welcoming others who seek freedom and opportunity. Look at the words by poet Emma Lazarus engraved on the base holding the Statue of Liberty:

"Give me your tired, your poor,
Your huddled masses yearning to
*   breathe free,*
The wretched refuse of your teeming
*   shore.*
Send these, the homeless, tempest-tost
*   to me.*
I lift my lamp beside the golden
*   door!"*

▲ Nicholas and Josephine Valeri, my great-grandparents, immigrated to the United States in the nineteenth century. All my great-grandparents were born in Italy, while their children—my grandparents—were born in the United States.

◄ The Statue of Liberty was a gift from France to the United States to celebrate our country's free and democratic traditions. It stands on an island in New York Harbor and was dedicated in 1886.

The Statue of Liberty is a symbol of hope, of a new start, recognized around the world. People have immigrated to America, to make a better life for themselves and their families, since the first European colonists arrived in the 1500s. Some of the earliest Europeans to explore and settle in what is now the United States included the Spanish, Dutch, and French. The Spanish founded St. Augustine, in what became Florida, in 1565. This is the oldest city on the U.S. mainland where people have continually lived. The first permanent English colony at Jamestown, Virginia, was not established until 1607.

"It lyes in a mild & temperate Clymate," William Byrd II wrote in 1736 about the colony of Virginia. "The woods are full of Buffalo's, Deer, & Wild Turkeys. . . . It is within the Government of Virginia, under the King [of England], where Liberty & Property is enjoyed, in perfection & the impartial administration of Justices hinders the Poor from every kind of Oppression from the Rich, & the Great."

"Any man or woman are fools that would not venture and come to this plentyful Country where no man or woman ever hungered or ever will,' Margaret McCarthy, who arrived in New York in 1850, wrote to her father in Ireland.

"We came over here with nothing but our bare hands," recalled Albertina di Grazia, who emigrated from Italy in 1913. "We were

dirt poor. This country gave us a chance to work and to get something out of our work and we worked hard for our children. And now they've got what we worked for. We're satisfied."

Immigrants who settle in the United States are grateful for the opportunities the country offers them. They are often welcomed, but Americans also have a long history of setting limits on immigration or rejecting it outright. George Washington, the first president of the

George Washington, the first American president, supported immigration of skilled workers and professionals to the United States, but he sometimes wrote against encouraging any new immigrants.

United States, sometimes supported immigration. But he also wrote, "I have no intention to invite immigrants, even if there are no restrictive [government] acts against it. I am opposed to it altogether."

Washington also wrote to John Adams, who would follow him as president: "[With] respect to immigration . . . that except of useful mechanics and some particular . . . men and professions, there is no use of encouragement."

Both of these ways of looking at immigration—openness to all or restrictions for some—are part of our heritage. In the early twenty-first century, we still debate who and how many people should be allowed into our country, and if and when they should be allowed to become citizens. Some Americans think of the United States as multicultural, made stronger by the diversity of different ethnic groups. Others think that there should be one American culture and that it is up to the immigrant to adapt to it. Still others have believed that some immigrant groups are incapable of adapting and should not be permitted to stay.

Americans whose families have lived here for some time—whether centuries, decades, or just a few years—often discount their own immigrant heritage. They look down on newcomers from other countries. Indeed, far from inviting Lazarus's "huddled masses," our laws, policies, and prejudices have often made it difficult for many immigrants to enter the United

States or to find themselves welcome when they are here.

This Land Is Our Land explores this country's attitudes about immigrants, starting from when we were a group of thirteen English colonies. Until the Chinese Exclusion Act of 1882, which kept Chinese workers from immigrating to the United States, there were no major national restrictions on immigration—therefore, there were no illegal immigrants, or what we now call "undocumented aliens": people from foreign (alien) countries who have no official papers to enter the United States. In the late nineteenth and early twentieth centuries, the biggest immigration issues were whether and how to limit the number of southern and eastern Europeans—and also to limit the immigration of Asians, who, in addition, were denied the right to become American citizens if they lived here.

Quota laws passed in 1921 and 1924 set limits on immigrants from Europe and Asia. Immigration from Latin America and Canada was not restricted then. As demands for labor in the southwestern United States increased in the 1920s, more Mexicans, especially, came to the United States. Some came officially; others came by simply crossing the border. The distinction between legal and illegal immigrants became important to Americans.

While the specific situations and attitudes toward some immigrant groups have changed,

Benjamin Franklin was a Founding Father of the United States, one of the authors of the Declaration of Independence. He admired Europeans, but he viewed the United States as a country of English customs and language and wrote against immigrants who kept their foreign ways.

of Aliens, who will shortly be so numerous as to Germanize us instead of our Anglifying them, and will never adopt our Language or Customs, any more than they can acquire our Complexion.

Now imagine the same words today, with "Mexican" substituted for "German."

As they came, settled, and endured, each immigrant group went through a remarkably similar experience. They left their countries to escape poverty, war, starvation, or religious and political persecution—or for economic opportunity. As foreigners who came from different cultures and often spoke languages other than English, they faced prejudice from groups that were already here. They seemed to threaten American customs and values established as early as the 1600s. Often, they were denied jobs and housing. They did the hardest and least well paid work. Yet they saved money and made homes here. Immigrant men brought over their wives and children; immigrant children brought their siblings and parents. Families reunited. Whole communities left their country of birth and regrouped in America. The children and grandchildren of immigrants, born here, spoke English. They absorbed American attitudes and ways of living. They grew in numbers and gained political power.

They often acted toward immigrant groups

the general ideas expressed for and against immigration remain remarkably constant. Look at what Benjamin Franklin wrote about the large number of German immigrants to Pennsylvania in 1751, more than two hundred and fifty years ago:

Why should the [German] Boors be suffered to swarm into our Settlements, and by herding together establish their Language and Manners to the Exclusion of ours? Why should Pennsylvania, founded by the English, become a Colony that came after them with the same kind of prejudice and discrimination that their families had encountered when they first moved here.

This Land Is Our Land does not attempt to answer all the questions and solve all the problems associated with immigration. Rather, it looks at our history to provide a context for discussion. If we examine the way Americans have responded to immigrants over time—and the responses have been startlingly similar and consistent—we gain an insight into immigration issues today. Why do we sometimes invite immigration and sometimes fear it? How much does race play a part in whether we accept new immigrants? Does the legacy of our country's origin as a group of English colonies still shape our attitudes?

This book also presents the experiences of immigrants who left their home countries to start a new life here. How did their expectations and aspirations match the realities of living in the United States? How was the experience of different groups affected by racial prejudice? How did they eventually succeed, if they did, in becoming Americans?

The title of this book is a play on the words of the 1940 song by folksinger Woody Guthrie, "This Land Is Your Land." For Guthrie, the United States was both *your* land and *my* land—the land of everyone who lives in this country, you and me. He is nonexclusive—meaning there is no one who does not belong here.

When we read the title *This Land Is Our Land*, what do we think "our" means? Is it *our* land, the land of the people who already live here, who were once but are no longer immigrants? Or is it *our* land, including the people who still come here for opportunity and freedom and to make the United States their home?

This Polish man, boarding a ship in 1907 to carry him to his new home in the United States, was one of millions of immigrants who hoped for a better life in this country.

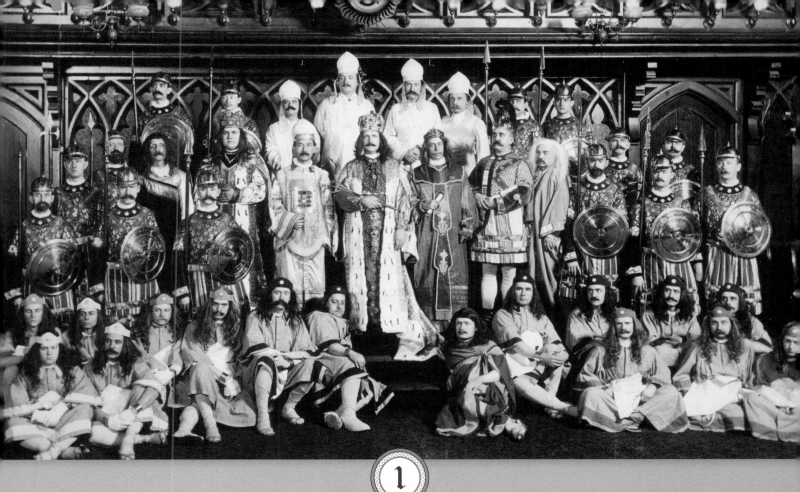

THE BEGINNINGS

GERMANS, IRISH, AND NATIVISTS

The United States thinks of itself as the world's "melting pot." It is the country where men and women of many nationalities can become united as Americans. J. Hector St. John de Crevecoeur, a French immigrant farmer, wrote in the late eighteenth century:

What then is the American, this new man? He is either an European or the descendant of an European. . . . He is an American, who leaving behind him all his ancient prejudices and manners, receives new ones from the new mode of life he has embraced. . . . Here individuals of all races are melted into a new race of men, whose labours and posterity will one day cause great changes in the world.

"America is God's Crucible, the great Melting-Pot where all the races of Europe are melting and re-forming!" Israel Zangwill wrote in 1908 in his play *The Melting Pot*. "Melting pot" became a popular term to describe the United States.

On the other hand, Americans have not welcomed—or have denied entry to—many groups of immigrants. Note that for de Crevecoeur and Zangwill, the ingredients in the melting pot were all European. Many of the first European settlers looked down on other peoples. They tried to enslave American Indians, fought them, and took over their land. They enslaved Africans; and even after all slaves were freed in 1865, black people were treated harshly and unfairly under legal segregation.

Many European Americans thought that Native Americans and African Americans were inferior to them, based on unscientific ideas about race. They thought they themselves were favored by God to rule over other peoples. Race was not just about looking different; it was about feeling superior to other groups of human beings. Feeling superior allowed Europeans to justify their treatment of others. Americans divided people into acceptable and unacceptable groups, depending on their physical features and countries of origin.

But when Europeans who were not English began to immigrate to the United States, they often encountered discrimination, too. The idea of race expanded to include those who were slightly darker than the descendants of most English people. Benjamin Franklin wrote "that the Number of purely white People in the World is proportionally very small. All Africa is black and or tawny [brown]. . . . And in Europe, the Spaniards, Italians, French, Russians and Swedes, are generally of what we call a swarthy [brown] Complexion; as are the Germans also, the Saxons [one group of Germans] only excepted, who with the English, make the principal Body of White People on the Face of the Earth."

Today nobody would think of Germans

and Swedes as not white. In fact, by the end of the 1800s, they were accepted as white and American. But deciding who could be American was more complicated than just skin color. It also had to do with English traditions of religion, culture, and language, and ideas about government. For many people, being American has meant being white, Protestant, and English-speaking.

Even in the early twentieth century, some American politicians, the press, and the public called for preserving the United States for English descendants, or what they called "Anglo-Saxons." (We might call them "Caucasian," or just "white people," today.) "Anglo-Saxon" was the name given to the English from the fifth to the eleventh centuries. (The Saxon settlers of England were actually German immigrants who pushed the Scots and Welsh out of England.) Americans thought of themselves as Anglo-Saxons if they were born in the United States and descended from an English immigrant. By the late 1800s, the descendants of German, Irish, Welsh, Scots, French, Swiss, Scandinavian, Dutch, and Belgian immigrants, who had sometimes faced discrimination, were also considered acceptable.

These people considered themselves "native Americans" (never mind that the only native Americans were the American Indians, who were here long before the Europeans). Those who opposed immigration by any other ethnic

group were called "nativists." Nativists didn't just believe that they were the only true Americans; they actively fought to keep other ethnic groups out of the United States.

Wherever the foreign-born population grew in numbers, nativism usually did, too. Two of the large immigrant groups following the founding of the English colonies were German and Irish. About 100,000 Germans

immigrated to America between 1710 and 1775, before the United States became a country. In fact, more immigrants arrived from Germany than from England during this period. Many came as indentured servants—mostly young people who were bound by contract to work for an American for several years in return for their passage, the cost of their transportation to the United States. The life was hard, and

families were sometimes separated. But this was also the eventual path to independence and even ownership of farms.

German and Irish immigrants made up two-thirds of new immigrants to the United States between 1830 and 1860. During this time, nativism was powerful in many parts of the United States, mainly on the East Coast. After 1840, Midwestern and Western states and territories actually encouraged immigration, since they had so much unpopulated land to be settled. Before the Civil War, some states, including Wisconsin, Michigan, and Indiana, even allowed immigrants who had started the process of citizenship, but were not yet American citizens, to vote.

The Irish came gradually until 1845, when Hannah Curtis wrote that "it is most dreadful the state the potatoes are in in Ireland . . . they are all tainted in the ground. . . . it is the opinion of every one there will be no potatoes. . . . we are greatly affraid there will be a famine this year." Many Irish, who depended on potatoes as their main food, died when the potato crops failed. From 1847 to 1852, almost a million people emigrated from Ireland, most to keep from starving. On April 2, 1852, the *New York Times* reported:

Many Irish came to the United States in the nineteenth century, especially after their potato crops—the main food eaten by the Irish poor—were ruined by disease beginning in 1845. These Irish are waiting for a coach in County Kerry, Ireland, to take them to a ship to sail for America in 1866.

On Sunday last three thousand emigrants arrived at this port. On Monday there were over two thousand. On Tuesday over five thousand arrived. On Wednesday the number was over two thousand. Thus in four days twelve thousand persons were landed for the first time upon American shores. A population greater than that of some of the largest and most flourishing villages of this State, was thus added to the City of New-York within ninety-six hours.

New York City was overwhelmed with immigrants in a very short time. So was Boston, where a city public health report described the slums where Irish immigrants lived, "huddled together like brutes, without regard to age or sex or sense of decency. Under such circumstances self-respect . . . all the high and noble virtues soon die out, and sullen indifference and despair or disorder, intemperance [drinking alcohol] and utter degradation reign supreme."

Nativists often used words like "brutes" to describe immigrants. Many white Americans had long described African Americans that way: as animal-like and less than human. This ugly racism was both the foundation and the legacy of slavery. The habits of racial thinking made it easy for nativists to feel prejudice against newcomers. People were judged by facial features as well as clothing, language, and the perceptions nativists had about the culture and values of the country they came from. These newer groups were seen as inferior and uneducated, the bearers of disease and crime.

But the Irish could and did become successful. "I am exceedingly well pleased at coming to this land of plenty," wrote an Irish immigrant to the *London Times* in 1850.

On arrival [in the United States] I purchased 120 acres of land at $5 an acre. You must bear in mind that I have purchased the land out, and it is to me and mine an "estate for ever", without a landlord, an agent or tax-gatherer to trouble me. I would advise all my friends to quit Ireland—the country most dear to me; as long as they remain in it they will be in bondage and misery.

What you labour for [here] is sweetened by contentment and happiness; there is no failure in the potato crop, and you can grow every crop you wish. . . . You need not mind feeding pigs, but let them into the woods and they will feed themselves, until you want to make bacon of them.

One of the main objections nativists had to some German immigrants (those who were not Protestants) and nearly all Irish immigrants was that they were Roman Catholic. The Catholic Church was led by the Pope in Rome, who some nativists believed wanted to take over the United States. "It is a fact, that Popery is opposed in its very nature to Democratic Republicanism; and it is, therefore, as a political system, as well as religious, opposed to civil and religious liberty, and consequently to our form of government," wrote Samuel F. B. Morse, in 1835. He was alarmed by the "increase of Roman Catholic cathedrals, churches, colleges, convents . . . in every part of the country; in the sudden increase of Catholic emigration [from Europe]; in the increased clannishness of the Roman Catholics, and the boldness with which their leaders are experimenting on the character of the American people." Morse was a prominent American, one of the inventors of the telegraph. Lyman Beecher, a respected Protestant minister and the father of the anti-slavery author Harriet Beecher Stowe, also expressed these views in the 1830s.

Germans (many settled on farms in the Midwest) also drew criticism for being un-American because they wanted to keep speaking German, send their children to German-language schools, and develop German-language newspapers—in other words, to keep their own culture. But most Germans began to adopt American ways as they settled in the United States and prospered economically.

"On this day I have purchased Wellington's farm for $1160," wrote William Seyffardt to his father in Germany in 1852. He had immigrated to Michigan. "The farm consists of 67 acres . . . [and] is the nicest location along the river. . . . I received a team of horses with harness . . . and eight tons of hay." He soon married Sophie Frank, another German immigrant. Seyffardt was pleased that German immigrants were coming together as a community. "The three

Roeser brothers are living . . . upward along the river. Otto Roeser (law student), the hunter . . . sometimes supplies us with deer meat. . . . Tomorrow will be the first German meeting concerning County affairs, and I hope that the Germans will take a more active part [in American politics]." The Seyffardts' oldest daughter asked when she was three, "Papa, are you writing to Germany?" He wondered, "I would like to know what her idea of Germany is." By that time, his Michigan village had a post office, a blacksmith shop, a hotel, and a mill, which he owned. Relatives who had settled in other Midwestern cities visited the family. They were becoming involved in American affairs. They were making a life here.

But by the 1850s, the American Party (or "the Native American Party," as they first called themselves) was successfully winning state elections. Opponents called them "the Know Nothing Party" because they wanted to keep the workings of their organization secret. Members therefore replied, "I know nothing," when asked about the party. One of the party's proposals was to extend the number of years before an immigrant could become a citizen to twenty-one; another would keep the foreign-born from holding an elected office.

Fear of foreigners is at the heart of immigration issues. When immigrants learn English, live among American citizens, and adopt an "American" way of living (as defined by nativists), they are said to be "assimilated"—they lose the habits and ideas that make them foreign and become part of general American society and culture. But if immigrants continue to live in their own communities and speak their own language, they make some Americans uncomfortable. Longtime Americans feel that they, not the immigrants, are living in another country, a world different from the one they grew up in. This feels threatening, especially if the newcomers—as many have through our history—come from poverty.

Laboring Americans believed that immigrants took jobs away because they were poor and desperate to survive. They would work for very low wages, and employers would hire them instead of native-born workers. Many did start out working for low wages, but with time they worked their way out of poverty and into better positions. "Only those who don't want to work don't like it here, since in America you have to work if you want to amount to anything," wrote Anna Maria Schano to her family in Germany in the mid-1850s. She lived in New York City. "You probably never thought I would be a washerwoman, but in America you needn't be ashamed if you work. . . . A person can have a hard time here at the start, but when someone's been here longer, then he can do well."

During the American Civil War (1861–65), American jobs and immigration were not important issues. Americans focused on

The American Party, known as the Know Nothings, was anti-immigration. This sheet-music cover, published in 1854, is dedicated to the party.

Many immigrants fought in the Civil War. More fought for the Union than for the Confederacy. This 1861 print shows the Garibaldi Guard on parade. Giuseppe Garibaldi was an Italian patriot and a friend of the United States. The soldiers in the Northern unit named after him were not only from Italy but also from Germany, Hungary, Switzerland, France, Spain, and Portugal.

whether the United States would remain one nation. In fact, immigrants from many countries fought for either the Union army or the Confederate army.

But anti-immigrant feelings thrived again after the war, when several economic depressions made it harder to find jobs. Again, nativists focused on Catholic immigrants. To be a member of the nativist American Protective Association, founded in 1887, one had to take an oath never to vote for a Catholic, never to give a Catholic a job when a Protestant was available, and never to go on strike with Catholics.

At the same time, Catholic immigrants and their children were becoming successful Americans. The Irish were gaining political power in New York and Boston. In 1885, Hugh O'Brien became Boston's first Irish-born mayor. He had come to the United States in 1832, when he was five. He became a publisher and a city legislator. He came before the potato famine in Ireland, but immigrants escaping the famine did much to elect him. He served for four terms.

Patrick Collins was Boston's second Irish-born mayor. When he was four, his father died. His mother could not support the family in Ireland; "the alternative, America, extended a hope that there would be opportunities for herself and her children," said a 1901 article published in the *New York Times*.

When Collins was twelve, "he became the office boy of a lawyer, and it was in this office that his dreams first began to take definite shape." He later apprenticed in an upholstery shop, and became foreman and then secretary of the union. He served in the U.S. House of Representatives from 1883 to 1889. "When not at his office," the *Times* wrote, "he can . . . be found at his home . . . deep in his books, which have been his teachers since he was obliged to leave school." Collins took office as mayor of Boston in 1902.

Collins had been a respectable leader in his trade union. Americans in general, however, worried about the rise of labor unions and of strikes, which were sometimes violent. Nativists

believed that most labor leaders—people who organized workers to demand better treatment and pay—were foreigners. They considered them "agitators"—people who stirred up trouble. Some immigrant labor and political leaders were anarchists, men and women who were against any organized government of laws. This frightened many Americans, who believed that if there were no government and laws, there would be chaos.

Some of the anarchists were German. Nativists blamed German labor agitators for the Haymarket Riots. On May 4, 1886, workmen demonstrated in Haymarket Square

Smoke from a dynamite bomb fills Haymarket Square in Chicago, where anarchists, many of them immigrants, demonstrated after several workers were killed in a strike. The 1886 Haymarket Riots turned many Americans against German labor leaders in particular.

in Chicago, protesting the killing of several workers the day before. Someone threw a bomb at police who tried to stop the demonstration. Several people died, and eight anarchists were convicted in a trial; four of them were executed. There was no strong evidence that any of them had thrown the bomb.

The anti-immigrant reaction was overwhelming. One article called the lead strikers "long-haired, wild-eyed, bad-smelling, atheistic, reckless foreign wretches, who never did an honest hour's work in their lives." Newspaper editorials said they were "Europe's human and inhuman rubbish" and "venomous reptiles." "There is no such thing as an American anarchist," another proclaimed. This connection of radical politics to immigrants continued for decades.

By the time of the Haymarket Riots, there was a new worry for nativists. Immigrants from England, Scotland, Wales, Ireland, and western European countries were not coming in great numbers. Instead, after 1870, a flood of southern Italian, eastern European, and Jewish immigrants caused Americans alarm.

These immigrants were generally poor and uneducated and tended to have what Benjamin Franklin had described as "tawny" skin. They were not considered white. "The color of thousands of them differs materially from that of the Anglo-Saxon," warned Congressman Thomas Abercrombie of Alabama.

"No one has suggested a race distinction," said Senator William E. Chandler in 1892. "We are confronted with the fact, however, that the poorest immigrants do come from certain races." Even the German and Irish immigrants and their descendants—who had finally been accepted in American society—saw the newcomers as foreign and dangerous. Racism was again in full flower—this was the same time that state governments in the southern United States were beginning to pass segregation laws against African Americans. The calls to restrict immigration became louder than the voices of opportunity and diversity.

2

ITALIANS, JEWS, AND EASTERN EUROPEANS

"The day came when we had to go and everyone was in the square saying good-bye. I had my Francesco in my arms. I was kissing his lips and kissing his cheeks and kissing his eyes. Maybe I would never see him again! It wasn't fair! He was my baby!" remembered Rosa Cassettari. She left Italy in 1884 to join her husband, who was already working in the United States. She was one of the millions of Italians—and tens of millions of Europeans—who immigrated to America between 1870 and 1924.

Almost all immigrants came with Rosa's vision: "America! The country where everyone could find work! Where wages were so high no one had to go hungry! Where all men were free and equal and where even the poor could own land!" Like Rosa, they often left behind children and spouses, fathers and mothers, or siblings. Families paid the passage for those they could afford to send, who were able enough to begin again in another country. And also like Rosa, many could only come in steerage—the cheapest way to travel by sea.

Steerage was famous for its harsh conditions.

All us poor people had to go down through a hole to the bottom of the ship. There was a big dark room down there with rows of wooden shelves all around where we were going to sleep—the Italian,

These steerage passengers gather on the deck of the *Patricia*, which sailed from France in 1902. In good weather, steerage passengers could leave their overcrowded quarters in the ship's hold for some light and air.

the German, the Polish, the Swede, the French—every kind. . . . The girls and women and the men had to sleep all together in the same room. The men and girls had to sleep even in the same bed with only those little half-boards up between us to keep us from rolling together. . . . When the dinner bell rang we were all standing in line holding the tin plates we had to buy . . . waiting for soup and bread.

When she arrived in New York Harbor, like most immigrants, Rosa waited aboard her ship. She did not come through Ellis Island—that famous immigrant processing center was not opened until 1892. She came through Castle Garden, an old fort at the tip of Manhattan, turned into an entry point in 1855.

The inside was a big, dark room full of dust, with fingers of light coming down from the ceiling. That room was already crowded with poor people from earlier boats sitting on benches and on railings and on the floor. And to one side were a few old tables where food was being sold. Down the center between two railings high-up men were sitting on stools at high desks. And we had to walk in line between those two railings and pass them.

"What is your name? Where do you come from? Where are you going?" they shouted.

Welcome to America.

Throughout much of the 1800s, state governments, instead of the federal government, were responsible for the entry of immigrants. New York opened Castle Garden to process the huge numbers that came through New York City. In 1882, Congress passed two immigration laws. One (the Chinese Exclusion Act) prohibited most Chinese people from coming to the United States (see chapter 3). The other, an immigration law for the states to carry out, charged fifty cents for everyone who entered the United States. It also set the first restrictions, which applied to Rosa. Incoming immigrants were to be examined "and if on such examination there shall be found among such passengers any convict, lunatic, idiot, or any person unable to take care of himself or herself without becoming a public charge . . . such persons shall not be permitted to land." A "public charge" was someone who could not support himself or herself but needed money or help from the government to live.

Rosa passed the examination, but American-born citizens from "desirable" backgrounds like English—and Irish and German—now

Jewish immigrants walk through Battery Park, in Lower Manhattan, about 1890. Some Americans complained that they took over the park, keeping American citizens from enjoying it in peace.

viewed immigrants like her, and those from eastern Europe, as intruders. "Numerous complaints have been made in regard to the Hebrew [Jewish] immigrants who lounge about Battery Park, obstructing the walks," reported the *New York Tribune* in 1882. "Their filthy condition has caused many of the people who are accustomed to go to the park to seek a little recreation and fresh air to give up this practice. . . . The police have had many battles with these newcomers, who seem determined to have their own way."

New York's genteel classes might have been annoyed, but American laboring men were furious. During an economic depression that lasted from 1883 to 1886, they were losing jobs. The owners of business and industry brought in contract workers from southern and eastern Europe to keep wages down. Coal miners in Pennsylvania accused owners who used Hungarian and Italian laborers of trying to "degrade native labor by the introduction of a class who, in following the customs of their ancestors, live more like brutes than human beings." During a Congressional session, the immigrant workers were described as "so many cattle, large numbers of degraded, ignorant, brutal . . . foreign serfs." Language like this—"brutes" (as the Irish had once been called), "cattle," and "degraded"—expressed the fear and hatred toward southern and eastern European immigrants.

In New York and other cities, these newer immigrants lived in their own neighborhoods. This was partly because, so far from home, they drew support from being near people from the same town or village. They spoke the same language and shared the same religious traditions. But it was also because many Americans did not want them to live in their neighborhoods.

When Rosa Cassettari joined her husband at an iron mining camp in Missouri, life was hard, but the German- and English-speaking people who lived nearby were friendly. However, when she moved to Chicago, there were apartments she couldn't have "because nobody would rent to Italians." At one point she and her family lived in a basement next to a factory. One night when it rained a lot, "my poor rooms had one foot of water in. The baby's cradle was swimming around, and that basket of clothes I used to wash, it was swimming around too. . . . My husband was throwing the water out with a shovel and sweeping it out with a broom."

Southern and eastern European immigrants were crowded together in poorly maintained tenements or other slum buildings in cities like New York and Boston. The housing wasn't cheap—landlords knew they had no place else to go. Many of the landlords were also immigrants from the same countries in Europe as their tenants, but they had been in

the United States longer. Some took advantage of the innocence and confusion of the newly arrived, guiding them to overpriced lodging and badly paying jobs.

Nativists believed that such foreign and strange people—living in isolation from the rest of Americans—could never be assimilated into American society. They could never "fit in" without their strangeness being noticed. They could never learn the customs, values, and language of the United States. Because some immigrants came to work and save money and then return to their own countries, nativists accused immigrants of taking advantage of America without giving back. Of course, by constructing roads, railroads, and buildings,

mining coal and iron, and producing textiles in factories, they were contributing to the United States while they were here. And although some never settled permanently, most did.

Sophie Zurowski emigrated from Poland to Indiana in 1895. "My husband worked in the steel mill all his life. Hard work. He was working hard. None of my boys ever went to work in the steel mill." One of them, who became a pharmacist, wondered to his father "how you could stand that place!" "If you want to make a living, you have to stand it," his father answered. Most immigrants were willing to do anything to succeed.

These women and a child in Old World dress have likely just come from Ellis Island. They were often met by relatives and friends who had already immigrated and could help them adjust to the United States. The photographer, B. G. Phillips, captured many images of Jewish immigrants like them.

Joseph Baccardo emigrated from Italy to Pennsylvania in 1898. When he was nineteen, he took over an unheated, poorly built barbershop. "[When] I'd saved some money, I had a concrete floor put down. Then I had plumbing put in—little by little; I didn't do it all at one time. I lived in the back. . . . I can still remember when my wife and I were married and we moved a little stove into the kitchen . . . and we had candlelight at night. We had a little farm, too . . . tomatoes, peppers, cabbage. . . . I did pretty well for myself and my wife helped me. . . . I'm eighty-nine . . . but I'm still cutting hair."

Nativists were not waiting for immigrants to become successful. By the 1880s, more and more Americans called for limits on their number. The Chinese Exclusion Act became law in 1882. At the same time, in Philadelphia, the National Home Labor League was founded "to preserve the American labor market for American workingmen." In New England, the American Economic Association announced a $150 prize for the best essay about "The Evil Effects of Unrestricted Immigration." The Haymarket Riots of 1886 called attention to foreign agitators with radical ideas about giving workers more power and changing American democracy. Americans later feared radicals from Russia and Italy.

But it was in the 1890s that a new era in immigration policy began. This was the era of Ellis Island—the entry point in New York Harbor, which for many is, along with the Statue of Liberty, the symbol of immigration to America. In fact, Ellis Island, which opened in 1892, came fairly late in the story of immigration. It was also, for many of the immigrants who passed through, a place of fear as well as hope, because with new government policies, they could be sent back to Europe without ever entering the United States.

The 1882 law was updated by the 1891

Ellis Island. New York City.

This 1915 postcard shows Ellis Island, opened in 1892 to process immigrants arriving in New York City.

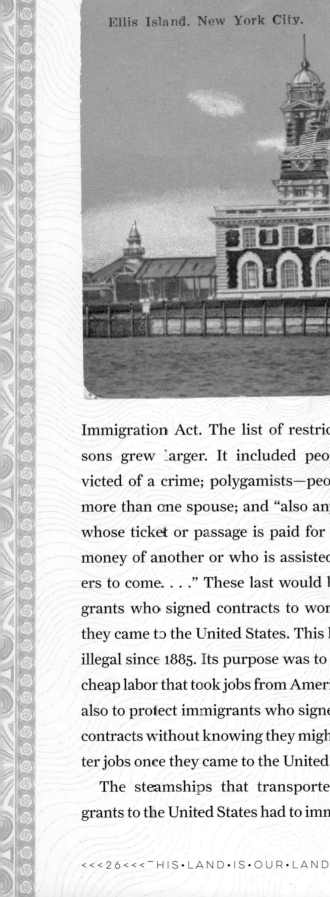

Immigration Act. The list of restricted persons grew larger. It included people convicted of a crime; polygamists—people with more than one spouse; and "also any person whose ticket or passage is paid for with the money of another or who is assisted by others to come. . . ." These last would be immigrants who signed contracts to work before they came to the United States. This had been illegal since 1885. Its purpose was to keep out cheap labor that took jobs from Americans but also to protect immigrants who signed unfair contracts without knowing they might get better jobs once they came to the United States.

The steamships that transported immigrants to the United States had to immediately take anyone who was rejected back to the port they had come from. Steamship companies had to pay a fine if they knowingly transported a person barred from entry. An immigrant who became a public charge within one year of his or her arrival could also be deported under certain conditions.

The 1891 act also created a new government job, a national superintendent of immigration. Immigration, which had been supervised by individual states, would be in the hands of the federal government.

Not every immigrant had to pass through Ellis Island. All those who came by steerage did. Those who traveled in second class or first class did not have to be inspected. Because they had enough money, they could land immediately in the city and begin their lives in the United States.

John Daroubian came through steerage. When he was sixteen, he emigrated from Armenia. "What are they going to do to us on Ellis Island?" he worried. "Many, many of our people were sent back. Some people were sent back because they couldn't speak right; some because they were sick. There was always something. I'm worrying, 'Will this thing work? What are we going to do? Will I get in? Will I get a job? Can I work?'. . . We got to Ellis Island and, thank God, we didn't encounter any trouble."

Faye Lundsky was only five years old when her family emigrated from Russia in 1893. They were escaping pogroms—

Many immigrants at Ellis Island were fearful of the eye examination. Authorities looked for trachoma, an eye disease that led to blindness. People with trachoma were sent back to their home countries.

Noted photographer and social reformer Jacob Riis took this photograph of the children's playground on the roof of an Ellis Island building in 1900. Immigrants who were waiting for inspections or because they were ill were fed and given beds, and their children enjoyed some recreation.

government-supported campaigns to persecute and kill Jews. She caught the measles on the steamship, "so when we landed at Ellis Island I was separated from my mother. They took me to the hospital where they kept those that were detained, and it was very frightening. I didn't know the language, and I didn't know what happened to my mother." She was finally allowed to join her family.

Most immigrants expected the United States to be "America, the promised land. Nuggets of gold hanging on Christmas trees, diamonds on the waysides, sparkling pearls in crystal water begging to be held by human hands," remembered Walter Lindstrom, who emigrated from Sweden in 1913.

But Lundsky pointed out, "My mother said

. . . there's an expression in Europe, 'America, the golden land.' She comes here and says, 'Where's the gold?' She saw people struggling . . . and it was a letdown for her. But as soon as he was able to, my father became a citizen and he would go and vote." Her father "was a sheet-metal worker. . . . He was jack of all trades. . . . He got any kind of job he could, and he struggled; it was very rough, but he made it on his own."

Hard work was a way of life for most immigrants. Not only men but wives and children as well had jobs. "We started work at seven-

Child labor was common not only among immigrants but also for other American children. This 1911 photo by Lewis Hine of the Mauro family shows the mother and her eight-, ten-, and eleven-year-old daughters sewing feather decorations in their New York tenement. The entire family earned $2.25 a week.

Immigrants settled in other places besides New York—they moved all around the United States. These immigrants are shrimp pickers in Mississippi in 1911. The youngest worker, standing on the box, is named Manuel and is five years old.

thirty in the morning, and during the busy season we worked until nine in the evening," recalled Pauline Newman, who came as a small child from Lithuania in 1901. She soon worked in a dress-making factory in New York. "They didn't pay you any overtime and they didn't give you anything for supper money. Sometimes they'd give you a little apple pie if you had to work very late. That was all.

"What I had to do was not really very difficult," continued Newman. "It was just monotonous. When the shirtwaists [blouses] were finished at the [sewing] machine there were some threads that were left, and all the youngsters—we had a corner on the floor that resembled a kindergarten—we were given little scissors to cut the threads off. It wasn't heavy work, but it was monotonous, because you did the same thing." Children like Newman were below the legal age for working. When city inspectors came to the factory, they hid in boxes.

Many Americans did not understand how much effort immigrants put in to be successful in the United States. Instead, they saw that immigrants lived in poor, crowded, dirty conditions. In many tenements there was only one toilet on each floor, and there were no windows in most of the rooms. Water had to be fetched from the yard. Four, six, or eight people might sleep in one room, and not on beds. Most of the money went for rent and some food. It was no wonder that they and their children had tattered clothes and shoes and that they caught diseases like tuberculosis. And, of course, they continued to speak their own languages.

But immigrants supported each other. "I remember we always had somebody living with us," said Lundsky, who grew up in Boston. "One person brought over somebody else; it was an uncle or a cousin, they had no place to go.... There was always room, even if it was on the floor. We were close with our neighbors. If anybody was sick, they would bring chicken soup."

Some Americans worked to improve immigrant living conditions. Settlement houses—community centers where social workers aided poor people in the city—helped new immigrants to find jobs and learn about health care, and they provided safe places for children to play. But their main goal was to Americanize immigrants from southern and eastern Europe as quickly as possible. They offered classes in English and in how to be a "good" American, which meant giving up foreign customs and languages. They encouraged immigrants to quickly become citizens.

But other Americans—and their voices were growing stronger—believed the solution to fighting slums, crime, and poverty was to severely restrict ethnic groups such as Italians, Jews, Poles, and Hungarians from entering the United States.

Nativists began to use what they believed were "scientific" arguments to support their calls for restriction. Anthropologists had begun to group people based on their physical characteristics, including skin color, size, and shape of the head. A new system of classi-

Johnny Yellow, a ten-year-old Polish immigrant, picks berries in Maryland, near Baltimore. This 1909 photograph is by Lewis Hine.

Anthropologists working in the late 1800s and early 1900s defined different ethnic groups by their "typical" physical characteristics. These heads, representing "types" from various countries, were sculpted to decorate the Library of Congress building.

fication, based on how people looked, divided Europeans into Nordic, Alpine, and Mediterranean categories. Nordics came from northern Europe (and, of course, England) and were superior to Alpines, from central Europe, and even more superior to Mediterraneans from countries like Italy, Greece, and Spain. This way of thinking associated physical traits with culture: people with lighter skin had superior cultures and values.

Nativists also used theories of biology—incorrectly—to support their claims. Charles Darwin had proposed that animals and plants evolved—grew and changed—over thousands of years. Animal and plant species that inherited the strongest traits from the preceding generations would be better able to survive. Americans speaking out against open immigration believed that poverty, crime, illiteracy, and other social ills did not grow out of limited economic and cultural opportunities. They believed these were inherited characteristics. Therefore, the

children of southern or eastern European parents would have no choice but to live in poverty. They would never become acceptable Americans.

"The hereditary character of pauperism and crime is the most fearful element with which society has to contend," asserted a social worker. Prescott F. Hall, a founder of the Immigration Restriction League in 1894, asked if Americans wanted their country "to be peopled by British, German and Scandinavian stock, historically free, energetic, progressive, or by Slav, Latin and Asiatic [Jewish] races, historically down-trodden . . . and stagnant."

Nativists worried that Anglo-Saxons—or Nordics, as they began to be called—would marry and have children with southern and eastern Europeans and Jews. These children would be weaker and less successful than "pure" Anglo-Saxons. These new immigrants threatened "to smother and obliterate American predominance, American influence, and American ideas and institutions," said one nativist society in the 1890s.

The first significant restriction law for

Europeans that nativists wanted was a literacy test. If men could not read or write in any language, they would not be allowed in. (Wives and children who could not read or write could enter with husbands and fathers who could.) Massachusetts Senator Henry Cabot Lodge led the drive in Congress to pass a law. In an 1896 speech, he said:

The illiteracy test will bear most heavily upon the Italians, Russians, Poles, Hungarians, Greeks, and Asiatics, and very lightly, or not at all, upon English-speaking emigrants, or Germans, Scandinavians, and French. In other words, the races most affected by the illiteracy test are those whose emigration to this country has begun within the last twenty years and swelled rapidly to enormous proportions, races with which the English-speaking have never hitherto assimilated, and who are most alien to the great body of the people of the United States.

Lodge believed that the literacy test would "shut out elements which no thoughtful or patriotic man can wish to see multiplied among the people of the United States."

Not every American wanted a literacy test to limit immigration. Owners of business and industry wanted to keep the flow of workers from Europe, whom they could pay less than American workers. Immigrants were also gaining political power as they became citizens; elected officials wanted to keep their vote. Some still believed that the United States should stay true to its democratic principles, providing opportunities for all. In 1897, President Grover Cleveland praised the "stupendous growth [of the United States] largely due

During World War I, immigrants from many countries fought for the United States. This 1919 poster asks all Americans to contribute money to the government to help pay for the war, which had just ended. On the right is a list of ethnic last names of soldiers, including O'Brien (Irish), Villotto (Italian), and Turovich (Russian).

to the assimilation and thrift of millions of sturdy and patriotic adopted citizens. . . . The time is quite within recent memory when the same thing was said of immigrants who, with their descendants, are now numbered among our best citizens."

Cleveland vetoed a congressional act requiring a literacy test in 1897. President William Howard Taft vetoed the literacy test act in 1913, and Woodrow Wilson vetoed it in 1917. But Congress overrode Wilson's veto, so the literacy test became law in 1917. Nativists thought it was a victory, but in fact the requirement kept out very few immigrants, including the law's target, those from southern and eastern Europe.

During World War I—which began in Europe in 1914 and which the United States entered in 1917—opinions about whether to restrict immigration changed again. The flow of immigrants from southern and eastern Europe slowed down. In addition, people from many ethnic backgrounds served in the United States military. An estimated 18 percent of the U.S. army was born in other countries. "These handicapped races [Italian and Russian, among others] are showing such loyalty, such devotion to our country, that we are realizing our former undemocratic, unchristian attitude toward them," declared a popular Protestant magazine in 1918.

When the United States joined England and France in the war against Germany, the question of loyalty became even more important. For a time, German immigrants and their descendants were feared and disliked, even though they had been accepted as Americans for decades.

Many Americans came to believe that if a person thought of himself as a German American, or Italian American, or Irish American—instead of totally an American—he or she could not be fully loyal to the United States. Former president Theodore Roosevelt said that all true Americans, no matter where they were born, should believe in "the simple and loyal motto, AMERICA FOR AMERICANS." But the idea of "100 percent Americanism" left little room for immigrants who could not adapt quickly to American ways.

The process of "becoming American" could be slow, but a lot of immigrants wanted to assimilate. Sonia Walinsky emigrated from Russia to Chicago when she was six years old. At school, "there was a program, and different children were supposed to do different things, and I was supposed to wave the American flag. I was very proud. I waved it . . . with all my might. I thought I was really an Americanka then."

But the war made Americans cautious about becoming involved in Europe's problems at the same time that large numbers of refugees from eastern and southern Europe wanted to immigrate to the United States. In addition, communists had taken over the government of Russia in 1917. Communists believed that the people of a community or country should jointly own all property, such as factories and farms. They should share equally with one another. But since this was hard for most people to do, it often meant that a communist government would set the rules and enforce them, not allowing anyone to disagree. Most Americans did not believe in this kind of government, so they were alarmed that immigrants promoting communism were in the United States. Some communists were deported, but the fear that political radicals would continue to come to the United States persisted. An economic depression in 1920 and 1921 increased American workers' fears of job competition.

Many Americans again believed that the way to keep America for Americans wasn't to Americanize immigrants but to keep them out. In 1921, there were enough votes in Congress to pass the first immigration act setting quo-

In 1909, Lewis Hine photographed these immigrant children at the Hancock School in Boston. Attending school helped children to learn the English language, as well as American ways.

Children who had to work during the day and adults attended night school to learn English, like this class held in Boston. Americans who feared that there were too many immigrants often did not realize how hard immigrants struggled to become American.

tas. (Quotas were an upper limit on the number of people who could come from each country each year.) It was called the "Emergency Immigration Act" because Americans were so worried about new immigrants flooding the country that they wanted to do something immediately to stop the flow. Congress set the total number of immigrants from all countries at 355,000 per year. (Almost 9.9 million European immigrants had come to the United States between 1905 and 1914—most from southern and eastern Europe.) Government officials counted the number of foreign-born people from each European country who lived in the United States according to the 1910 census. They said that 3 percent of that number could come from each country each year.

Although the number of immigrants dropped significantly in 1921, nativists still thought the quotas for eastern and southern Europeans were too high. They feared that jobs would be taken away from Americans; that communists, labor agitators, and other radicals would enter the United States; and, most important, that too many immigrants could not be assimilated—"The old Americans

For a few years in the early 1900s, Americans believed that immigrants could be "Americanized" if they attended classes about citizenship and language, like this one held for Jewish women in New York City. But by the early 1920s, many Americans believed that there were too many immigrants to assimilate into an American way of life.

Men attended this Americanization class in New York in 1920. By 1924, quota laws would severely limit the number of immigrants from southern and eastern Europe.

are getting a little panicky, and no wonder. . . . America, Americans and Americanism are being crowded out of America," wrote a reader to the *New Republic* in 1924.

Albert Johnson, a congressman from Washington State, headed the House of Representatives' committee on immigration. He led the fight for tougher quotas. He said:

Today, instead of a well-knit homogeneous citizenry, we have a body politic made up of all and every diverse element. Today, instead of a nation descended from generations of freemen bred to a knowledge of the principles and practice of self-government, of liberty under law, we have a heterogeneous population no small proportion of which is sprung from races that, throughout the centuries, have known no liberty at all. . . . In other words, our capacity to maintain our cherished institutions stands diluted by a stream of alien blood, with all its inherited misconceptions respecting the relationships of the governing power to the governed. . . . It is no wonder, therefore, that the myth of the melting pot has been discredited. . . . The United States is our land. . . . We intend to maintain it so. The day of unalloyed welcome to all peoples, the day of indiscriminate acceptance of all races, has definitely ended.

Congress passed the Johnson-Reed Act in 1924. Instead of using the 1910 census to decide America's foreign population, it used the census of 1890. This was because in 1890 there had been more northern and western European immigrants and fewer southern and eastern European immigrants living in the United States than in 1910. Congress wanted the United States to return to its English roots, which meant having immigrants from Britain (or western and northern Europeans) be recorded as the largest group in the population. The law set the quota at only 2 percent (instead of 3 percent) of immigrants from each country living here in 1890. The total number of immigrants would be only 150,000 a year. New immigrants from southern and eastern Europe would make up only 15 percent of the total each year.

It took five years before the details of all the quotas were worked out. After July 1, 1929, the yearly quotas for northern and western European countries included:

GREAT BRITAIN (England, Wales, and Scotland) **AND NORTHERN IRELAND**	**65,721**
IRISH FREE STATE (now Ireland)	**17,853**
SWEDEN	**3,314**
NETHERLANDS	**3,153**
FRANCE	**3,086**
NORWAY	**2,377**

The yearly quotas for eastern and southern European countries included:

POLAND	**6,524**
ITALY	**5,802**
CZECHOSLOVAKIA (now the Czech Republic and Slovakia)	**2,874**
RUSSIA	**2,784**
HUNGARY	**869**

After 1870, *millions* of immigrants had arrived from these countries. After 1929, only 869 Hungarians and 5,802 Italians could immigrate each year. Great Britain and Northern Ireland (the country known as the United Kingdom) was allowed almost 66,000 per year, but English, Irish, Welsh, and Scottish immigrants never reached this number.

With the 1924 Immigration Act, racial assumptions became law. Americans believed that they were preventing their country from being taken over by inferior groups of human beings who could never change. Country quotas were not eliminated until 1965.

But the 1924 act was focused mainly on Europeans. Asians, who came even lower on the Anglo-Saxon scale of desirability, had more prejudiced and restrictive policies aimed at them. Starting in the late nineteenth century, the United States passed laws that would not only limit their entry but also never allow them to become American citizens.

③

THE OTHER SHORE

IMMIGRANTS FROM ASIA

"I happened to see a Western movie, called *Rodeo*, at the Golden Horse Theater in Okayama City," said Frank Tomori, who was born in 1907 in Japan, "and [I] was completely obsessed with 'American fever' as a result of watching cowboys dealing with tens of thousands of horses in the vast

Western plains. Enormous continent! Rich land! One could see a thousand miles at a glance! Respect for freedom and equality! That must be my permanent home, I decided." Tomori eventually immigrated to the United States. He ran a laundry in Portland, Oregon.

Frank Tomori described a vision of the United States held by people from all over the world. Immigrants from Asia were among them. Chinese, Japanese, Filipino, Korean, Indian, and other Asian peoples came to America for economic opportunity and personal freedom.

Asians, like Europeans, often left their home countries because of extreme poverty. "There were four in our family, my mother, my father, my sister and me," explained a Chinese immigrant in the nineteenth century. "We lived in a two room house. Our sleeping room and the other served as parlor, kitchen and dining room. We were not rich enough to keep pigs or fowls, otherwise, our small house would have been more than overcrowded.

"How can we live on six baskets of rice which were paid twice a year for my father's duty as a night watchman? Sometimes the peasants have a poor crop then we go hungry. . . . Sometimes we went hungry for days. My mother and me would go over the harvested rice fields of the peasants to pick the grains they dropped. . . . We had only salt and water to eat with the rice."

◀ In the late 1860s, Chinese immigrants provided much of the labor to build railroads connecting the eastern and western United States. Here they are laying track in Nevada.

The first large Asian group that came to the United States was Chinese. These men (the vast majority of Chinese immigrants were men) came as early as 1849. They were drawn by the California Gold Rush. Between 1849 and 1930, some 380,000 Chinese immigrated to the United States. The majority of those who came to mine gold, and those who arrived later to build railroads, work on farms, and open shops, lived in California.

After the Civil War, the Central Pacific Railroad began building track in California to join the Union Pacific Railroad, linking the eastern and western United States. Although Irish immigrants and others worked on the railroad, Chinese workers were especially important in the West. The railroad owners believed that Chinese men worked harder and were more dependable than other immigrants and Americans, and they worked for less pay. At one point, Chinese made up at least 80 percent of the Central Pacific Railroad workers. Most of them intended to return to China after earning enough money, but many remained in the United States.

Although the owners of mines, railroads, and farms considered Chinese people excellent workers, white workers saw them as a threat to their jobs. White politicians objected to their presence. The majority of Chinese people lived in California, and California tried harder than any other state to limit Chinese immigration.

"[The] concentration, within our State limits, of vast numbers of the Asiatic races, and of the inhabitants of the Pacific Islands, and of many others dissimilar from ourselves in customs, language, and education" threatens American mining, reported the California Assembly as early as 1852. This was only three years after Chinese people had begun to arrive in significant numbers.

Racial alarm grew worse in California. "Certain it is, that the greater the diversity of colors and qualities of men, the greater will be the strife and conflict of feeling," wrote Hinton Helper in *The Land of Gold*, published in 1855. The same year, the California legislature passed "An Act to Discourage the Immigration to This State of Persons Who Cannot Become Citizens Thereof." It taxed shipowners $50 for every person landed who was not eligible to become a citizen of the United States.

The question of citizenship went back to 1790, when Congress passed a naturalization law. ("Naturalization" is the process by which a citizen of one country becomes a citizen of another. It applies only to immigrants.) The law

Many Chinese who stayed in the United States settled in San Francisco. Here two children stand on a sidewalk in that city's Chinatown. Arnold Genthe, another noted photographer, took the photograph some time between 1896 and 1906.

stated "that any Alien [foreigner] being a free white person, who shall have resided within the limits and jurisdiction of the United States for the term of two years, may be admitted to become a citizen thereof." In 1798, Congress changed the law so that immigrants had to live here for five years. But it did not change the phrase "free white person." In 1870, Congress passed a naturalization law that allowed "aliens of African nativity" and "persons of African descent" to become citizens. Africans and African Americans were added to ensure that no previous law could stand in the way of their having the rights of citizens granted to them by the Fourteenth Amendment (1868) to the Constitution. The Fourteenth Amendment (and the 1866 Civil Rights Act before that) was the first national law to say that anyone born in the United States—whether or not their parents are citizens—is an American citizen.

The laws of 1790 and 1870 did not say that people from Asia could not be citizens. It did not mention them at all. But because they were not mentioned, the United States government did not allow Chinese and other Asians to go through the process of becoming citizens. When a few Asians tried to become American citizens in the early 1900s, the Supreme Court said they could not, arguing that only white and black people were covered by law. It wasn't until the 1940s that Asians from some countries were allowed to become citizens.

There were a so many Americans who supported immigration to the United States. In 1871, cartoonist Thomas Nast shows a woman who represents America, scolding Americans who oppose Chinese immigration. "Hands off, gentlemen! America means fair play for all men," she reminds them.

Finally, in 1952, an immigration and naturalization law removed the barriers to all Asians gaining American citizenship.

In 1869, work on the first railroads that joined the eastern and western United States ended. More than 10,000 Chinese railroad laborers were out of work and looking for other jobs. White Americans panicked. "The 60,000 or 100,000 Mongolians [Chinese] on our Western coast are the thin edge of the wedge which had for its base the 500,000,000 of Eastern

As the number of Chinese immigrants increased, so did opposition to them. In 1886, this cover of *Puck*, an American humor magazine, showed a man representing the state of Oregon shooting at and killing Chinese men who wanted to come there. The cartoonist was James Wales.

Despite discrimination and violence, the Chinese population grew. In this Arnold Genthe photo, Chinese "children of high class" walk in San Francisco. Chinese merchants and businessmen petitioned the state of California to provide education for their children, "so that they may learn the English language."

Asia," wrote economist Henry George in the *New York Tribune* in May 1869. He predicted that millions of Chinese would come here and take over the country. "The Chinaman can live where stronger than he would starve. Give him fair play and this quality enables him to drive out stronger races." George's article is full of prejudices, incorrect assumptions, and exaggeration. It portrays Chinese men as weaker than white Americans, then argues that they can live on practically nothing.

Chinese immigrants came together to protest against such prejudice and discrimination. Many of them were successful businessmen in California and intended to stay there. Around 1878, 1,300 Chinese, including the leaders of the Chinese Merchants of San Francisco and California, petitioned the state about a law that did not provide schools for their children. These men paid American taxes.

We respectfully represent that these sections of the law very clearly exclude our children from the benefits of the public schools, and we humbly approach you . . . begging you to change these laws, so that our children may be admitted to the public schools, or what we would prefer, that separate schools may be established for them. We simply ask that our children may be placed upon the same footing as the children of other foreigners so that they may learn the English language, which would be for the advantage of all.

In 1885, the law was amended to provide separate schools "for children of Mongolian or Chinese descent."

People from China were the first group to have national laws passed against their immigration. Congressmen from California and other Western states campaigned for these laws. Senator Aaron Sargent was one of the most vocal lawmakers to speak out against Chinese immigration in the 1870s. The Page Act of 1875 prevented the entry of Chinese forced workers—those imported to work as slave labor, which was allowed in other countries. The law also kept out prostitutes—Congress outrageously believed this would keep out almost all Chinese women. Therefore, many more men than women emigrated from China.

Many Americans believed that no matter how educated or wealthy Chinese immigrants were, they could never become integrated into American society. This group of cartoons in an 1880 issue of *Puck* frightened readers with images of Chinese "invaders" taking over cities throughout the United States.

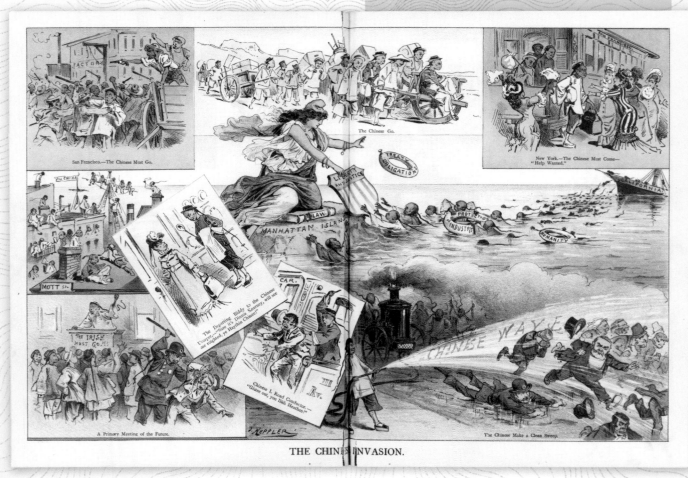

THE CHINESE INVASION.

Senator John Miller of California became the leading anti-Chinese spokesman in Congress in the 1880s. He proposed drastic legislation to limit Chinese immigration. In 1882, Congress passed the Chinese Exclusion Act, allowing no Chinese laborers to enter the United States for ten years. It called for deporting any Chinese laborer who had entered the country after November 17, 1880, and specifically declared that no Chinese person could become a citizen. Congressmen from western states—where the majority of Chinese people lived—voted for the act. Southern Congressmen did, too. Although few Chinese lived in the South, racism there against African Americans and other people of color was strong. Eastern states in general did not support the Chinese Exclusion Act, although Chinese lived in eastern cities and encountered racism. The Geary Act of 1892 extended exclusion for another ten years. In 1902, the barriers to immigration of Chinese laborers were made permanent by another law.

With the passage of the 1882 Chinese Exclusion Act, immigration became a national issue. This was ten years before Ellis Island opened. Before 1882, immigrants who came from both Europe and Asia had to be inspected by a Customs Service officer. Customs are taxes on all the things a person brings in from another country—including jewelry, furniture, rich fabrics like silk, wine, and fruits and vegeta-bles. Collecting customs taxes was a way for the U.S. government to control trade. After the 1882 Immigration Act was passed, inspectors could also keep out people with diseases or who had no way to support themselves. They also began to collect a fifty-cent "head" tax, a charge for each immigrant who entered the country.

But the U.S. government had no system in place to keep Chinese workers from entering. The first patrols along the Mexican border by government officials in the 1890s were aimed not at keeping Mexicans out but Chinese

people who might try to illegally enter by land. There was also a patrol on the border with Canada for the same reason: not to keep Canadian immigrants out but to prevent Chinese from entering.

Some Chinese people could still come to the United States, including diplomats, merchants, and laborers who had been here before 1880 and were returning from visits to China. There had to be some way to let these people in and

Angel Island, shown here about 1910, when it opened, processed immigrants arriving in San Francisco. Not only were Chinese and Japanese inspected here, but, later, Indians, Russians, and people from the Pacific Islands.

still enforce the no-workers law. The first Chinese people to come after the Chinese Exclusion Act were held on unused ships in San Francisco harbor while U.S. officials decided whether they could enter the United States. (Some of the ships also held people who had the highly contagious disease smallpox.) The shipping companies that transported immigrants were responsible for paying for food and other expenses while they were being held. In 1898, the largest shipping company, the Pacific Mail, turned one of its office buildings on a San Francisco pier into "the Detention Shed," where those who wanted to immigrate had to wait. The *San Francisco Call* newspaper wrote that the space was "not much bigger than an ordinary four-roomed cottage. Yet . . . no less than 357 Chinamen . . . were confined. . . . There they were, squatting on the floor around boxes and bundles of all kinds." The *Call* later noted, "There are men in this place who have been detained for weeks and months owing to some defect in their papers." Wong Hock Won, a Chinese man held in the Detention Shed, wrote, "Here you are cramped and doomed never to stretch. You complain that the shed leaks and they [the guards] say, 'Why should you care?'"

Even the white press understood that the conditions were bad. In 1905, Congress approved money to build an immigration center on Angel Island in San Francisco Bay.

By 1915, the number of Japanese immigrants passing through Angel Island outnumbered the Chinese. Immigrants were asked hard and detailed questions about their family history. Here, in 1923, a young Japanese man is interviewed by U.S. government officials, who will decide if he can enter the country.

U.S. government officials decided who could or could not enter the United States from Asia. But the two immigration centers were different in several ways. Twelve million immigrants came through Ellis Island in the sixty-two years it was open; fewer than half a million people stopped at Angel Island during the thirty years it was open.

Perhaps the biggest differences were that most Europeans were accepted and their stays at Ellis Island were short. Fewer Asians were admitted through Angel Island and their stays were much longer. Some were held for years. They lived in dormitories like army barracks, men and women separately. Those who had official documents to prove they were the children of U.S. citizens could enter fairly quickly. But "paper sons and daughters," who might have forged documents, were asked tough questions by American officials. For example, they had to describe in detail the village their father came from and who their ancestors were.

Some Asians held on Angel Island carved their names and dates into the walls. Some

It finally opened in 1910 and was used until 1940. It processed not only Chinese but also people who wanted to emigrate from more than eighty countries. The largest group to be held there was the 122,000 Chinese, but there were 63,000 immigrants from Japan, and 7,000 Sikhs from India. Even 12,000 Russians who lived in the far eastern part of their country (near Japan and Alaska) went through Angel Island.

Angel Island has often been called "the Ellis Island of the West," because it was there that

Chinese people carved sad or bitter poems. The carvings are still there. One Chinese person wrote:

I used to admire the land of the Flowery Flag [the United States] as a country of abundance.

I immediately raised money and started my journey.

For over a month, I have experienced enough wind and waves. . . .

I look up and see Oakland [California] so close by. . . .

Discontent fills my belly and it is difficult for me to sleep.

Many Chinese spent months or even years held on Angel Island. Some eventually entered the United States. Others were forced to return to China. While they waited, a few of them carved poems in Chinese into the walls, describing their journeys, loneliness, discouragement, and desperation.

I just write these few lines to express what is on my mind.

But as Chinese immigration slowed down, immigrants came from other Asian countries. By 1915, more Japanese than Chinese were processed on Angel Island. Japanese had begun coming to Hawaii in the 1880s and to the mainland (California, Oregon, Washington State) in the 1890s. They, too, were escaping impoverished lives. "What strikes me most is the hardships paupers are having in surviving [in Japan]," wrote a Japanese journalist in 1885. "Their regular fare consists of rice husk or buckwheat chaff ground into powder and the dregs of bean curd mixed with leaves and grass."

Japanese immigrants also had visions of opportunity. One wrote a haiku poem:

Huge dreams of fortune
Go with me to foreign lands,
Across the ocean.

Japanese immigrants found work in mining, railroad building, and lumber mills, or as servants in the homes of white people. But the majority quickly

Like immigrants at Ellis Island, immigrants coming through Angel Island had to have medical examinations. Here American officials are examining a group aboard the ship *Shimyo Maru* before they land on the island.

became farmers, especially growing fruits and vegetables they could sell in cities. Many Japanese families earned enough money to own their farms. But, as with the Chinese, American workers saw Japanese workers as competitors. Americans, especially those living on the Pacific Coast, believed they were being flooded by an "alien race." In 1901, California governor Henry Gage called Japanese immigrants a "menace" to American workers that was as dangerous as the "peril from Chinese labor" had been.

American politicians and newspapers rarely talked about people like Chiura Obata, who came in steerage from Japan in 1903. He and his shipmates "went through the medical examination," he reported when he wrote home about landing in Seattle, Washington.

The customs officials noted that most of my belongings were art supplies. . . . We went into town, had a meal of beef and Japanese cabbage for 10 cents. We got a room for 20 cents each and found it large enough. . . . Later, after going to a Japanese bathhouse, we heard there was a Baptist minister . . . who would

"Picture brides"—Asian women who came to marry Asian immigrants—saw only their future husbands' photos before they met them. Here a group of Japanese picture brides arrives on Angel Island.

take us in.... Pretty decent—lots of Caucasians there. Tonight was the first time I had slept in a bed in a house in North America.

Obata became a professor of art at the University of California at Berkeley.

Racism against Asian immigrants in the early 1900s took the same form as it did throughout the country: sometimes laws separated ethnic groups, and, where there were no laws, discrimination often resulted in racial segregation. The Native Sons of the Golden West, a California organization of white nativists, challenged: "Would you like your daugh-ter to marry a Japanese? If not, demand that your representative in the Legislature vote for segregation of whites and Asiatics in the public schools."

An attempt in 1906 to segregate Japanese children in schools set off an international crisis. Again, this happened in California, where the majority of Japanese immigrants lived. The San Francisco Board of Education ruled that "all Chinese, Japanese, and Korean children [be sent] to the Oriental Public School." While many Americans throughout the country were against Japanese immigration, the Japanese government had military power. The federal government, led by President Theodore Roosevelt, did not want to offend Japan. And the Japanese government was upset by this act of racism.

Roosevelt wanted to ease tension. He got San Francisco to take back the segregation order; he also persuaded the Japanese government to forbid Japanese laborers to leave Japan for the United States. This was called "the Gentlemen's Agreement" of 1907. However, "picture brides"—Japanese women coming to marry Japanese men they had never met—and other family members of those already here were allowed in.

The Gentlemen's Agreement stopped the flow of workers from Japan, but it did not stop discrimination and violence against the Japanese in America. "The persecutions became intolerable. My drivers were constantly attacked on the highway," said the Japanese owner of a laundry. "My place of business [was] defiled by rotten eggs and fruit; windows were smashed several times." In 1913, California passed a law that "aliens ineligible for cit-izenship" could not own land. It did not specify Japanese—or Chinese, or Koreans, or other Asian immigrants, for that matter—but it was only Asians who could not become citizens.

Other states, mainly western and southern, passed laws that kept Asians from buying land. They included Oregon, Washington, Utah, Wyoming, Montana, Arizona, New Mexico, Texas, Idaho, Arkansas, Florida, Louisiana, and Minnesota. It wasn't until 1952 that the Supreme Court declared that alien land laws were unconstitutional.

Although Japan was an ally of the United States during World War I, anti-Japanese feeling continued. Many Japanese immigrants were Buddhist. More than Catholicism in

Japanese immigrants who were Buddhist often upset Americans who did not understand the religion. Here worshippers gather at the Hompa Hongwanji Buddhist Temple in Los Angeles, around 1925.

the nineteenth century, Buddhism seemed foreign and threatening to Americans. "Our mission is to elevate the spiritual life, not to dictate politics or policies of any government," explained Buddhist bishop Koyu Uchida in 1920 to a U.S. House of Representatives committee on immigration. "We should also like to point out that Buddhism is Democratic, an ideal long held by the citizens of the United States. . . . The [Buddhist missionaries trained in Japan] are required to have sufficient knowledge and information of America and American customs before being sent here, and are requested to perfect themselves as soon as possible after their arrival."

Efforts like this, which were designed to help Americans understand foreign cultures, did not seem to matter. After the 1924 Immigration Act went into effect, the United States would accept only one hundred immigrants each from Japan and China per year. These had to be eligible for citizenship, and Asians could not become citizens. This meant, in effect, that Europeans living in Asia could fill the quota.

Filipino immigrants—

people from the Philippines—faced a different situation. The United States acquired the Philippines after defeating Spain (which had owned the Philippines as a colony) in the Spanish-American War (1898). Filipinos then fought the United States for their independence but became an American territory in 1902. Because of this, Filipinos were allowed to immigrate to the United States without restrictions, even after the quota law of 1924 went into effect. They came by ship straight from the Philippines, and sometimes from Hawaii, landing at ports on the Pacific Coast, including San Francisco and

Many Filipino immigrants worked on farms and helped with harvests, like this migrant worker in California in 1935.

Portland, Oregon. After they passed through a customs check, like American citizens, they could enter the country.

Still, their lives were not easy. Many worked in seasonal farming, moving from place to place to pick and can fruits and vegetables.

"[My friend] Ninang and I cut spinach, we cut off the roots," wrote fifteen-year-old Angeles Monrayo in 1928. "Oh, first we pick out the bad leaves and the yellow then cut off the roots and put the spinach leaves on a wide moving-belt. We are paid 20 cents a crate for every crate we finish. Today I finish 10 crates only, so I made $2.00 exactly. . . . The women are all pieceworkers, especially the spinach cutters. The women who have been working in the cannery every year works faster and so they make more money. Me . . . I am glad that I am working and that I made $2.00 today." Three months later, drying apricots, Monrayo wrote, "I don't know how long the fruits will last. I know I am going to work as long as they [the land owners] keep us."

Filipinos suffered the same discrimination that Chinese and Japanese immigrants did. In Stockton, California, where Angeles Monrayo lived, police patrolled the streets at night to keep Filipinos from entering the white neighborhoods. Signs on hotels read POSITIVELY NO FILIPINOS ALLOWED.

In 1934, Congress made the Philippines a commonwealth with a Filipino government (effective in 1935). At the same time, it reduced the number of Filipinos who could immigrate to the United States to only fifty per year, another sign of racial discrimination. (The Philippines became fully independent from the United States in 1946.)

Koreans and Indians immigrated to the United States in much smaller numbers. After Japan occupied Korea in 1905, Koreans came to Hawaii. About one thousand immigrated to the U.S. mainland. Mary Paik Lee and her family were agricultural migrants. She was six years old when she came to the United States. In Riverside, California, she lived in a "camp . . . of one-room shacks, with a few water pumps here and there and little sheds for outhouses." The shacks had been built for Chinese railroad workers in the 1880s. Her "first day at school was a very frightening experience. As we [she and her brother] entered the schoolyard, several girls formed a ring around us, singing a song and dancing in a circle. When they stopped, each one came over to me and hit me in the neck." Not knowing the Paik family was Korean, the American students sang as though she were Chinese:

Ching chong, Chinaman,
Sitting on a wall.
Along came a white man,
And chopped his head off.

"The last line was the signal for each girl to 'chop my head off' by giving me a blow on the neck," wrote Paik. Moving to northern California, the Paik family encountered more prejudice. But in Claremont, California, Paik had her "first experience with the American way of living. The new house . . . had several rooms with beds. . . . The kitchen had a gas stove, electric lights, and a sink with faucets for cold and hot water. . . . For the first time, I felt glad that we had come to America."

Living in the United States was a combination of opportunity and discrimination. Paik stood up to her high school history teacher. "When we came to the pages about China and Japan, he referred to them as the lands of 'stinking Chinks and dirty Japs.' . . . [He] said that Korea was a wild, savage country that had been civilized by the 'Japs.' That was the last straw. . . . I walked up to him and said, 'Where did you learn Asian history? You don't know a thing about the subject.'"

Younghill Kang was a Korean who came to the United States in 1921, before passage of the immigration act. As a teenager he was interested in European and American science and culture. "I studied with . . . concentration and enthusiasm. . . . I studied with all the self-denial and earnestness of my father. . . . I studied with all the brains of my many ancestors who had been scholars and poets and officials beyond count or number. . . . I began to learn the law of gravitation. . . . The study of the lives of Lincoln and Napoleon, and the geography of the World kindled my enthusiasm until sometimes I seemed just to be dazzled by stars in the head," he wrote in the novel *The Grass Roof* in 1931. Kang became a professor at New York University.

Immigrants from India came with the same desire to improve their lives. "Do you wonder

In 1918, Raymond Song Herr, a Korean American, played football for YMCA College (now Aurora University) in Illinois. Often the children of immigrants learned English and assimilated into American society more easily than their parents.

These Sikh immigrants from India work on a railroad in Oregon. They seemed especially foreign to many Americans because they wore turbans on their heads.

when you look at India, with its low wages and high taxes, its famines and plagues, its absence of all incentive toward advancement, that the dam which for so long has held the people in check is weakening?" asked an article in *Pacific Monthly* magazine in 1907. "Do you wonder that the East Indians are turning their faces westward toward the land of progress and opportunity?"

But by 1920, only about 6,400 immigrants from India had come to the United States. Despite their small numbers, some Americans worried that they were too different to become true Americans. "The civic and social question concerns the ability of the nation to assimilate this class of Hindus and their probable effect upon the communities where they settle," stated an article titled "The Hindu,

the Newest Immigration Problem" in *Survey* magazine. "Their habits . . . their lack of home life—no women being among them—and their effect upon standards of labor and wages, all combine to raise a serious question as to whether the doors should be kept open or closed against this strange, new stream."

The question was answered by the Immigration Act of 1917. Passed by Congress over President Woodrow Wilson's veto, it banned specific kinds of people, including "idiots" and "criminals," from entering the United States. It also created the "Asiatic barred zone," which prevented immigration not only from India but from most of Asia and the Pacific Islands as well. The "Asiatic barred zone" was a powerful symbol of American prejudice and racism. (In 1946, the Luce-Celler Act allowed Asian Indians and Filipinos to immigrate to the United States—but only one hundred a year! It also, finally, made Asian Indians and Filipinos eligible for citizenship.)

The experience of Asian immigrants in Hawaii was different from that of those who came to the U.S. mainland. More than 300,000 people from China, Japan, Korea, and the Philippines came between 1850 and 1920. Many started out as contract workers in the sugarcane fields run by American companies. The life was hard. "We worked like machines," said one laborer. "We were watched constantly." A Korean woman remembered a foreman who "would gallop around on horseback and crack and snap his whip."

Because the workers came from different countries in Asia, they often lived in separate communities. It was difficult for them to organize for workers' rights. But in the early 1900s there were some successful strikes. More and more Asian immigrants decided to make Hawaii their permanent home. Others moved from there to the Pacific Coast states.

Although Hawaii became a U.S. territory in 1898, it did not become a state until 1959. Racism was a factor. By 1920, Asians made up 62 percent of the population. But after World War II, American attitudes began to change. There is a higher percentage of people living in Hawaii who are Asians or their descendants than in any other state.

Perhaps the most controversial discrimination against an Asian group in the United States occurred during World War II (1939–45). Fighting had already begun in Asia and Europe. In December 1941, after Japanese troops bombed the American base at Pearl Harbor in Hawaii, the United States went to

Many Asian immigrants first lived in Hawaii before they came to the U.S. mainland. Here workers load sugarcane onto a train, about 1905.

These Japanese Americans are leaving Los Angeles for an internment camp in 1942, after the U.S. government called for isolating them from other Americans because the United States was at war with Japan.

When Japanese people—both immigrants and American citizens—had to leave their homes, they also had to leave or sell their possessions. These Japanese fishing boats in San Pedro, California, are for sale.

war against Japan. Many in the Pacific Coast states believed that the Japanese would attack them. They also believed that Japanese immigrants (called "Issei") and their American-born children (called "Nisei") sabotaged the American war effort. California, Oregon, and Washington pressed for action against them. On February 19, 1942, President Franklin Roosevelt issued Executive Order 9066, calling for Japanese Americans living within one hundred miles of the Pacific Ocean to be interned in camps. (In Hawaii, which had a large Japanese population, only a small number were interned. Most Japanese immigrants and their descendants were too important to the islands' economy, including agricultural production.)

American-born Monica Sone, whose parents were Japanese immigrants, remembered a family member going "to the Control Station to register the family. He came home with twenty tags, all numbered '10710,' tags to be attached to each piece of baggage and one to hang from our coat lapels. From then on we were known as Family #10710." Sone wrote the 1953 autobiography *Nisei Daughter*.

Between 1942 and 1945, 110,000 Japanese Americans, including citizens like Sone, were removed from their homes (many lost their homes and possessions) and were imprisoned in rough internment camps. Most of the camps were in the desert. "No houses were in sight, no trees or anything green—only scrubby sagebrush and an occasional low cactus, and mostly dry, baked earth," described an internee named Yasui.

The United States was also at war with Germany and Italy, but only a few thousand Germans and Italians were interned, and they were released before the Japanese were. Racism and prejudice clearly played a part in the decision to intern Japanese Americans. Despite this action, many Japanese Americans volunteered and fought for the United States in World War II.

Other Asians have immigrated to the United States since then. The numbers were small until the 1970s, when Vietnamese and other Southeast Asians fled the results of war and political persecution. Prevented from coming to the United States for years, Asians nonetheless became one of the two groups who make up the majority of immigrants to this country in the first decades of the twenty-first century. Latin Americans are the other group.

Internment camps were usually located in desolate desert places, like this "relocation center" in Manzanar, California.

SOUTH OF OUR BORDER

LATIN AMERICAN IMMIGRANTS

In the 1980s, Jorge and Sara Garcia brought their twelve-year-old daughter, Vanessa, and their eleven-year-old daughter, Paola, from Bolivia to the United States. They worked hard. Jorge traveled on long bus rides to take jobs as a commercial painter, away from his home for days at a time.

Their goal was for their daughters to have a better life than they had in Bolivia. The girls, too, were encouraged to work hard. "Some Americans don't see the opportunities they have here. They take things for granted," said Paola. "Our parents taught us that if we wanted something, we had to fight for it."

Vanessa applied to attend George Washington University as she was finishing high school. "The day I opened that [acceptance] letter, I knew my life would be different. It justified everything my parents had been through." Vanessa became a finance manager, and Paola became a physical therapist. In 2013, their parents became U.S. citizens. "When the ceremony was over, I cried and cried," recalled Sara Garcia. "I thought to myself that now I have everything I want. I am an American citizen, both my daughters are professionals and the future is ahead of them. What more could I ask of life?"

Like European and Asian immigrants before them, the Garcias expected that life in the United States would be difficult but also worth all the sacrifices they made. They are Hispanics—people who come from the countries that were once Spanish colonies in the New World, including Mexico, most of Central America, and parts of South America and the Caribbean. They are also known as "Latinos" because they come from Latin America. They speak Spanish, and their culture is a mix of Spanish and Native American traditions.

(Native Americans, including the Inca and the Maya, lived in South as well as North America.) Brazilians, who speak Portuguese, are also considered Latinos, but not Hispanics.

Although Americans tend to group "Hispanics" together, Mexicans, Colombians, Puerto Ricans, Cubans, and others from Latin America come from different cultures, with different histories and different traditions. It is only because they speak Spanish that they are classed together. For some Americans today, the fact that Latin American immigrants continue to speak Spanish makes them seem unable to assimilate and unwelcome in the United States.

Latinos experience a great deal of discrimination, just as African Americans, Asians, and southern and eastern Europeans have. Yet when polled, they continue to have more faith in the American Dream of personal struggle and success for their children than many whites and African Americans.

Latinos are at the center of a debate about whether they should be allowed to settle here and/or become citizens, because many of them enter the United States illegally. This means that they have not applied for visas. Visas are documents that let them stay in the United States for a period of time but not permanently—for example, to visit family, study at a college, or be tourists. (Actually, not just Latinos but people from many countries stay in the United States illegally, often by simply not leaving when their visitor or student visas expire.)

For more than 150 years after the United States was founded, no immigrants from Latin America were illegal; they were not even counted as part of the 1924 Immigration Act. Ranchers and farmers in the Southwest wanted their labor.

The area of the United States where most Latinos first enter—the American Southwest, including Texas, Arizona, New Mexico, and California—was once owned by Mexico. After the Mexican-American War (1846–48), the United States gained a large part of this territory. An estimated 80,000 Mexicans lived there. They were given the right to stay or to go to Mexico. If they stayed, the government promised that they could remain Mexican citizens but still own their property.

The great majority of Mexicans who remained in the territory, however, decided to become American citizens. Interestingly, the heritage of a fair number of them was all or part Native American. Yet the white Americans living there usually accepted them. In fact, it was common for white men to marry the daughters of wealthy Mexican American ranchers. Still, Mexican Americans did suffer from some discrimination in their new country.

The original Mexicans in California and Texas called themselves "Californios" and "Tejanos," respectively. Now Mexicans living in the United States are known as "Chicanos."

Before the 1960s, most Latino immigrants were from Mexico. Some Chicanos came to settle; some came for seasonal work. They moved easily back and forth across the border until World War I. In 1910, when the Mexican Revolution began, there was a surge of emigrants who fled war and economic hardship. Fighting continued until 1924. Between 1910 and 1929, some 700,000 Mexicans immigrated to the United States.

The Battle of Buena Vista was fought in Mexico in 1847 during the Mexican-American War. The United States gained much of the Southwest after the war.

During the Mexican Revolution, which began in 1910, many Mexicans suffered from the devastation of war. They sought safety in the United States, like this group, which crossed the desert on horseback sometime between 1910 and 1915.

How did they enter? They could cross the land border on foot, by car, or on a train. If they passed through an inspection station, they could be let in or turned away by customs officials. Mexicans crossing the Rio Grande used bridges or ferries. In the early twentieth century, immigrants were inspected not only by customs but also by immigration inspectors. The cities and towns on the border where U.S. officials check Mexicans and other Latinos are called "ports of entry." By the 1920s, there were already at least twenty-four legal ports on land to check people coming to the United States from Mexico. By 2014, there were forty-seven ports of entry on land, in California, New Mexico, Arizona, and Texas. The busiest port of entry in the world is at San Ysidro, California, where people cross from Tijuana, Mexico, into San Diego. Many Americans also cross from San Diego to Tijuana to visit Mexico. El Paso, Texas, has many ports of entry to different parts of the city as well. Immigrants can also arrive by ship and, since the 1950s, fly into airports, where they have to pass customs and immigration inspections. But there are miles and miles of land and river crossings where there are no inspection stations.

Ernesto Galarza was eight years old when his family left central Mexico for Sacramento, California, in 1910 to escape the effects of revolution. They lived in the poorest part of town. "Lower Sacramento was the quarter that people who made money moved away from. Those

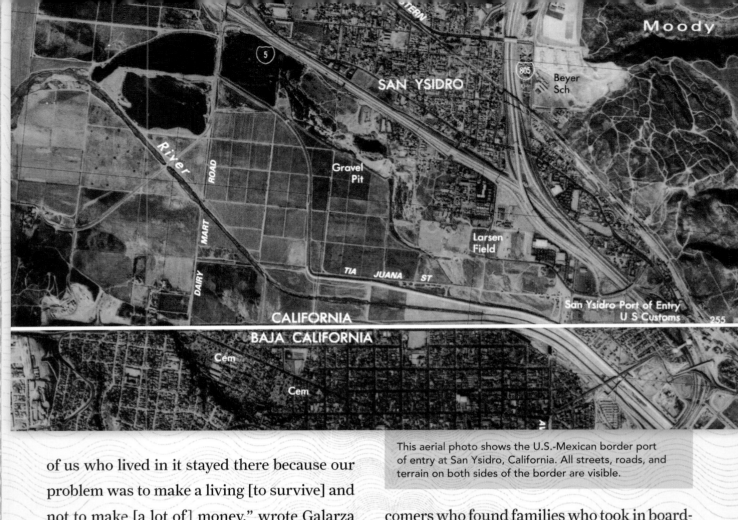

This aerial photo shows the U.S.-Mexican border port of entry at San Ysidro, California. All streets, roads, and terrain on both sides of the border are visible.

of us who lived in it stayed there because our problem was to make a living [to survive] and not to make [a lot of] money," wrote Galarza in *Barrio Boy*, based on his life story. "A long while back . . . there had been stores and shops, fancy residences, and smart hotels in this neighborhood. . . . When the owners moved uptown, the backyards had been fenced off and subdivided, and small rental cottages had been built in the alleys in place of the stables."

Galarza saw conditions grow worse as more immigrants came. "The *colonia* [neighborhood where Mexicans lived] was like a sponge that was beginning to leak along the edges, squeezed between the levee, the railroad tracks, and the river front. But it wasn't squeezed dry, because it kept filling with new-

comers who found families who took in boarders; basements, alleys, shanties, run-down rooming houses and flop joints where they could live." But Galarza went to high school and college and earned a graduate degree. A professor and poet, he became a leading labor activist, organizing farm workers.

Most Mexicans worked on farms. American employers badly wanted their labor. In the 1900s and 1910s, many found year-round work on large farms. They settled in the United States. But in the 1920s, fewer and fewer stayed in one place; they became migrant workers, moving from place to place to harvest cotton, fruit, and vegetables. They might earn as little as $1.50 a day. Their labor was wanted, but they were thought to be socially and culturally inferior. Even when they did not live in Chicano communities—for example, in El Paso, Texas—they were isolated from other Americans.

In 1924, Congress passed the Johnson-Reed quota law (see chapter 2). There were no quotas established for immigrants coming from Latin America (or from Canada). But the Johnson-Reed law did set up rules for the way people could enter the United States. They needed visas, had to pass medical examinations and literacy tests, and had to pay a tax.

The first official U.S.-Mexico Border Patrol was established in 1924 to keep immigrants from entering where there were no immigration inspection stations. Mexicans who had

This Mexican migrant laborer weeds between cantaloupe plants in the Imperial Valley, California, in 1937. His pay was thirty cents an hour.

The U.S.-Mexican Border Patrol was formed in 1924 to keep immigrants from entering the United States except through official ports of entry. More than ninety years later, some agents still ride horses where motor vehicles can't go. These men from the McAllen (Texas) Horse Patrol Unit are searching along the border in south Texas in 2013.

freely been going back and forth for years were confused by the new requirements. Getting the right papers also cost more money than hiring a "coyote"—a person who smuggles people—to take someone illegally across the border. "The total cost, head-tax plus visé [visa], is eighteen dollars. On both sides of the border there are 'coyotes' who for five dollars arrange that the [phony] documents be attained very quickly," wrote the Mexican anthropologist Manuel Gamio in a study published in 1930. So some Mexicans began to come without papers or with forged papers, because they could still find work and make more money in the United States than they could at home. They came because American farmers and ranchers in the Southwest wanted their labor.

Valente Ramírez remembered crossing the Rio Grande to work in Texas in the 1920s, when the difference between legal and illegal Mexican immigrants was still hazy. "They [the Texas Rangers] helped us cross because they wanted workers from Mexico. . . . The next day we found work [at the mines]. We were standing near the office when we were asked to go to work right away. But they did not pay very much—10 cents per hour, but not 10 cents in money, rather they gave us chits and you took them to the store [owned by the employer] and bought your groceries." Ramírez stayed in the United States. He was still living in Los Angeles in 1972.

Ramón Lizárraga came to the United States in 1903. He worked as a musician for two years, then went back to Mexico. In 1926, he returned to California, buying a car—a Model T Ford. There were still no quota restrictions that kept him from coming. He drove back to Mexico, sold his farm, and drove his wife and children to Los Angeles to settle permanently. Like Ramírez, he was still living there in the 1970s.

During the Great Depression of the 1930s, there was not enough work for anyone, American or immigrant. People with a Mexican heritage—even those who were American citizens—were targeted in raids and roundups. Over 400,000 Mexicans and Mexican Americans (some say over one million) were encouraged, bullied, or forced into returning to Mexico. (This is called "repatriation"—returning immigrants to their native countries.)

In 1943, Mexicans and African Americans ride a truck to Corpus Christi, Texas, where they work on farms.

In the 1940s, however—even before the United States entered World War II in 1941—industry and farm production increased, and more workers were needed. The United States and Mexico started the Bracero Program—"bracero" means someone who works "using his arms," a manual worker. The program allowed Mexican laborers to work in the United States for short periods of time. They would have contracts that guaranteed them a fair wage and decent working conditions. Only men could come; they could not bring wives and families. The first braceros came to the United States in 1942. The program lasted until 1964.

In 1955, braceros were supposed to earn 50 cents per hour. In Mexico, farm laborers earned about 65 cents a day. Aureliano Ocampo left his home in a small town in Mexico to travel to Edinburg, Texas. His contract allowed him to work from May 11 to June 8, 1955, packing tomatoes and melons. He was placed in a house with other braceros. It was "in poor condition and very dirty. We didn't have a chance to clean it as we arrived after dark. We didn't sleep good because of the condition of the cots."

These braceros wait for trains to take them to Arkansas, Colorado, Nebraska, and Minnesota to harvest beets in 1943.

Each man was supposed to receive $1.15 a day to buy his own food. Instead, six braceros were given $3.19 to share. They were paid 30 cents an hour, rather than 50 cents, for their work.

Some braceros returned to Mexico or arranged illegally to work with other farmers when they found bad conditions. Mexican immigrants who came without proper documents were insultingly called "wetbacks," because they supposedly swam the Rio Grande to enter the United States. "As a wetback, alone, safely across the border, I may find a farmer who needs one man," said Carlos Morales. "He will pay me honestly, I think. But as a bracero,

Braceros were not allowed to bring families, but other Mexicans immigrated with their wives and children. The Vigues family lived in a public housing development planned for African Americans in Austin, Texas.

I am only a number on a paycheck . . . and I am treated like a number . . . not like a man."

American ranch and farm owners liked using bracero labor; they could keep wages low. This upset American laborers who could not find jobs at decent wages, and they blamed the Mexican immigrants. In the 1950s, farm wages rose all over the United States, except in the areas where braceros worked. Anti-Mexican sentiment was usually strongest where most Mexican immigrants lived—the American Southwest and California. (In the twenty-first century, states such as Arizona, Texas, and California have tried to pass their own laws dealing with immigrants, including denying state government benefits to undocumented residents.) The Bracero Program was supposed to stop undocumented immigrants from coming to the United States. Instead, the number increased. Men who did not have the money and time to get papers through the Bracero Program, or who were not accepted because the number of braceros was limited, or who wanted to come with wives and families, came anyway. Some traveled beyond the Southwest, getting higher-paying jobs in cities like Chicago. And some moved back and forth between Mexico and the United States, sometimes legally and sometimes not.

"The next time I came over I had papers, and I worked in the fields for a while," said José Garcia, who first immigrated in 1959 to California. "But then I got this job in the mushroom plant. The main reason I like it is it's less heavy work and it's more steady. I've been here ten years now. Of course, they favor the Anglos in the plant. They give them the easier job. They don't like Mexicans to touch the machinery, you know. Where I work, if they had the custom of carrying things on a burro [a small donkey], they wouldn't let the Mexicans touch the burro."

Like the early German, Irish, southern and eastern European, Jewish, and Asian immigrants before them, Mexican immigrants were met with fear and prejudice.

In 1954, Joseph M. Swing became commissioner general of the Immigration and Naturalization Service (now the U.S. Citizenship and Immigration Services), which governed immigration. He believed that an "alarming, ever-increasing, flood tide" of undocumented immigrants was "an actual invasion of the United States." He authorized Operation Wetback, "a direct attack . . . upon the hordes of aliens facing us across the border." Many, but not all, were living in the Southwest. The operation also deported workers from southeastern states, as well as from northern cities where they worked in industry. From 1953 through 1955, Operation Wetback located and

Border Patrol agents in El Paso, Texas, check under a train for smuggled immigrants in 1938.

sent back to Mexico more than 800,000 undocumented immigrants. At the same time, more Mexicans signed up for the Bracero Program in this period, but undocumented immigrants kept coming, too.

What happens to immigrants who are deported after they've been living in the United States for years, and what happens to their children? "Their home life was [suddenly] broken, they were compelled to sell homes [and] possessions at a great sacrifice, their incomes ended and they were picked up by the Border Patrol at night and 'dumped' on the other side of the river in numbers so great [that] Mexico's railways and bus lines could not move them into the interior [of Mexico] fast enough," said one Texas resident about a 1950 deportation drive. "Thousands of these families were stranded along the border destitute without food or funds or employment."

Americans often grouped all Mexicans together—longtime legal immigrants, American citizens, and undocumented aliens—and looked down on them with fear that they would take their jobs or were criminals. Even American citizens of Mexican heritage experienced discrimination.

Tomás Rivera was born in the United States in 1935 to Mexican migrant workers, who worked everywhere from Texas to Minnesota. He wrote a novel about his life from 1945 to 1955. His young character "needed a haircut, so he went into the barber shop. . . . But then the barber told him that he couldn't cut his hair. . . . He thought the barber didn't have time, so he remained seated waiting for the other barber. . . . But this barber told him the same thing. That he couldn't cut his hair. Furthermore, he told him that it would be better if he left. He crossed the street and stood there . . . but then the barber came out and told him to leave." Tomás Rivera became a respected novelist, poet, and educator. He was the first Chicano to hold one of the highest positions in the University of California system, as the chancellor at the Riverside campus.

The Bracero Program ended in 1964; with mechanized farming and new technology, farms needed fewer human workers. But undocumented immigrants keep arriving. In 1990, Cesar Millan, who was twenty-one, "was trying to cross [the border] from Tijuana." He met a man who said he could take him across. "The coyote charged me one hundred dollars. For me, that was God sending me somebody to tell me to cross because I was already trying for two weeks and no luck."

While he tried to earn the money, Millan explained, "To survive you sweep floors, you ask for food, they see you're dirty. Some people give you tacos, some people say no, but you can survive because your adrenaline is feeding you, and somehow your body conserves whatever you eat. I ate tortillas. I ate whatever people gave me because I wanted to save [money]. . . . I slept in the street. The street was my house."

Cesar Millan became a famous dog trainer in the United States, known as "the Dog Whisperer." He has had his own television shows. Millan became a U.S. citizen in 2009. "Mexico is my mother nation, but America is my father nation because America gave me the direction that I should take," he said. "So how do I feel about finally being part of a country that I'm in love with? I have a great amount of appreciation because my children were born here . . . and the world got to know me here. It was hard to touch my dreams, but this is the place in the world where dreams come true."

Although immigration from Mexico is most often in the news, immigrants come to the United States from South and Central America and Spanish-speaking Caribbean islands as well. They come to achieve a better life. "I am rising in my job," said Jaime Alvarez, who emigrated from Peru in 1971.

I am foreman of the cleaning staff for the whole floor [in the hospital]. . . . And I have applied to be assistant to the director of maintenance. He says I have a good chance of getting the position, because I speak both English and Spanish and can talk with the employees who speak very little English. Almost all our new workers here at the hospital are from Latin countries, and they start out knowing nothing—not even the words for broom or soap. Everything must be translated. That's how it was for me, too, four years ago. But I went to school, and now, maybe, I will get a better job because of it. And then my family will come over and our dreams will be true.

Large numbers of people from Puerto Rico come to the United States. The island was owned by Spain until its defeat in the Spanish-American War in 1898. Like the Philippines, Puerto Rico became an American territory; it is now called "the Commonwealth of Puerto Rico." All Puerto Ricans were granted U.S. citizenship in 1917, if they live in the United States. (If they stay in Puerto Rico, they do not have all the benefits of American citizenship.) Those who come to this country are technically not immigrants. Yet they have faced much discrimination and often struggled to make a living. Many are black, so they experience prejudice both as Hispanics and as black people.

Piri Thomas's mother was Puerto Rican, and his father was Cuban. He grew up in East Harlem in New York City in the 1930s and 1940s. When he was thirteen years old, "the weather turned cold one more time, and so did our apartment. . . . The cold, plastered walls embrace that cold from outside and make

▶ Cuban refugees sailed this small boat to Miami, Florida, in 1962.

Aurora Flores sits on the lap of her grandfather Don José Flores, who plays traditional Puerto Rican songs on his accordion. Many Puerto Ricans, like Flores, grew up in New York City but celebrated their cultural traditions.

it a part of the apartment, till you don't know whether it's better to freeze out in the snow or by the stove." His mother told him, "I like los Estados Unidos [the United States], but it's sometimes a cold place to live—not because of the winter and the landlord not giving heat but because of the snow in the hearts of the people."

The first Puerto Ricans who came to the United States found it hard to break out of poverty. Piri Thomas was angry, turned to crime, and spent seven years in prison. He got his high school degree there and began to write. His autobiography, *Down These Mean Streets* (1967), became a classic. He spent much of his life trying to help young people at risk.

Many Puerto Ricans embraced family and cultural customs as they adapted to the United States. They took pride in their heritage. Aurora Flores remembered the first time her grandfather played the accordion: "My mouth opened and my eyes widened as I heard life breathe from the crinkled accordion skin. . . . This music took me to where I came from. It helped me understand the traditions of my grandparents. It gave me the strong foundations that helped me survive. . . . No matter where I was born or what language I speak, I am *Boricua* . . . a Puerto Rican in New York." Flores is a writer, composer, and leader of a salsa band.

Immigrants also come to the United States from Central America. Some have emigrated because their governments changed, taken over by military leaders or run by dictators who did not tolerate opposition. Some have come to escape violence. There are Latin Americans who emigrated to escape political persecution and even death, including those who have come from Nicaragua and El Salvador. They sought asylum—a safe place—in the United States. They were refugees, a different kind of immigrant, with their own stories to tell.

SEEKING SAFETY AND LIBERTY

REFUGEES

"I decided to come here because there is freedom of thought and expression," said a Cuban named Alejandro, who escaped to the United States when he was twenty-three. Cuba is an island ninety-three miles off the coast of Florida. In 1959, Fidel Castro took over the government, and Cuba became a communist nation. The United States denounced the communists and broke off political relations. Many Cubans who were anti-communist fled the island and were welcomed in the United States.

Few were allowed to leave Cuba legally, so on September 21, 1979, Alejandro and four other young men "lowered [a] boat into the water" at two a.m. "Our clothes were dark so that they would not attract attention. . . . When we started, we did not even know how to row. One oar went one way and the other another way. . . . Finally we caught on to the rhythm of rowing. . . We rowed all day Tuesday and then all the next day and night," coming closer to Florida. But the group ran into a storm and found themselves back near Cuba, without food and little water. They reversed and on the fifth day were picked up by an American. "He gave us some food, and divers in another boat gave us some sandwiches, apples and Coca-Cola," recalled Alejandro. In Miami, they were issued temporary papers. It was the start of their lives as refugees in the United States.

Refugees are a special kind of immigrant. They can no longer live safely in their home countries "because of persecution or a well-founded fear of persecution on account of race, religion, nationality, membership in a particular social group, or political opinion." That was the definition used in a 1980 law that allowed refugees to immigrate to the United States. People can also face danger in their home countries if they are women or homosexuals. Persecution can mean that people who criticize their government, or another ethnic group or religion—or who just belong to another ethnic group or religion—can lose their jobs and homes and/or be imprisoned, tortured, and even killed.

Some of the early colonists who settled in the land that became the United States came because they were not allowed to practice their religions freely. These included the Puritans in New England and the Quakers in Pennsylvania. Others came because they opposed—and sometimes rebelled against—their governments. But the United States did not have separate laws for refugees who wanted to immigrate until the 1940s. (Before that, they might have come in under the regular quota laws but could not come automatically or immediately because they were in danger.) Even specific laws for refugees did not make it easy for many of them to enter the United States.

During and after World War II, there were millions of refugees who had been forced to flee their homes in Europe and Asia. Jewish people were a particular target for the Nazi government in Germany and Austria and the other European countries Germany took over. They were sent to concentration camps—prison camps with especially harsh and even cruel conditions—and most did not survive. They were the victims of genocide—an attempt to kill an entire ethnic group, which can mean millions of deaths.

In the late 1930s, the United States government could see the danger Jews were in. President Franklin Roosevelt and some members of Congress expressed concern, but little was done to change the immigration laws or bring refugees to the country in large numbers. Myron C. Taylor, who led the U.S. delegation to an international conference on political refugees in 1938, assured Americans that "our plans do not involve the 'flooding' of this or any other country with aliens of any race or creed." In 1939, the German ship *St. Louis*, which was carrying 933 refugees, was not allowed to land in the United States. Most of the passengers were already on the quota list but had not been fully processed. The ship was forced to return to Europe, and many of the passengers died during World War II.

Elise Radell, an eight-year-old German girl who was Jewish, was accepted by the United States. She remembered what happened to her home on November 9, 1938. The S.S., a German paramilitary group, "pushed us aside and came into the house. . . . they went about this utter destruction with axes. . . . [The] china closet was knocked all over and the pictures on the wall . . . and the furniture all just went. . . . The pillows were ripped and the feathers . . . just flew all over the house."

This anti-Jewish violence destroyed thousands of businesses, temples, and homes. The night of November 9–10 came to be called *Kristallnacht* ("Crystal Night," or "the Night of Broken Glass") because of all the glass fragments from broken windows littering the

Jewish refugee children, on their way to homes in Philadelphia in 1939, wave at the Statue of Liberty.

streets throughout Germany. Radell's father was one of some 30,000 Jewish men sent to concentration camps at that time, but he was released. The family was determined to flee.

"You couldn't get a visa to America unless you had relatives there," said Radell. "I think Roosevelt could have tried to open the quota a little bit. Maybe he did try; I don't know. But we had an aunt who had come to the U.S. in 1936. . . . We finally managed to get the visas . . . and we got on a boat and landed here in August 1939. . . . My father got a job in a fabric store as a stockboy [in Newark, New Jersey]. He had owned a large textile firm in Ludwigshafen. Now he earned eleven dollars a week."

The United States did take in some refugees before the end of 1941 (when it entered the war) and did relax some requirements. The country was not alone in turning down Jewish refugees. France, which accepted them freely until 1933, began tightening its policies. England did not take many Jewish refugees. Some fled to Palestine, an area of the Middle East that the League of Nations gave to England to control after World War I and that later became the country of Israel. England closed it to refugees in 1939. Turkey accepted Jewish refugee scientists, and the Philippines and Shanghai, China, were other Jewish refugee destinations.

It is true that in the 1930s the United States and its allies could not have foreseen the horror of mass executions to come. But anti-immigrant and anti-Jewish sentiment in many countries—and, in the United States, sticking to the principles of the quota law—meant that six million European Jews found no refuge and died at the hands of the Nazis.

After World War II, there were millions

of "displaced persons" who were not living in their home countries. Some were able to return, but many sought refuge in emigration. The United States had fought the war to gain freedom for all people in Europe and Asia. Many Europeans wanted to come to the United States. But almost no Asian refugees came during this period. There were still restrictions on Asian immigration and the ability to become citizens in the United States. A significant number of Asians chose to immigrate to Australia or stayed within Asia itself. Although southern and eastern Europeans were becoming accepted as Americans in the United States, there was still racism against African Americans, who lived under segregation. Opposition continued against accepting nonwhite and Jewish immigrants, who, some Americans thought, could never assimilate.

The biggest issue that affected how Americans felt about immigration, however, was the growing number and increasing power of communist governments. The Soviet Union (U.S.S.R.), an American ally during World War II, was communist; so were the countries of eastern Europe, including Poland, Czechoslovakia, and Hungary, that the U.S.S.R. had been given control of after World War II. Mainland China formed a communist government in 1949, and communists were gaining power in Southeast Asia. The Cold War between communist countries (mainly the U.S.S.R. and later China) and democratic countries (mainly the United States, as well as countries of western Europe, including England and France)

World War II devastated much of Europe and left millions homeless. These children from the village of Rabka, Poland, wear the ragged clothing they have left after the war.

lasted until the early 1990s. It was a "cold" war because there was no major, direct fighting between the United States, western Europe, the U.S.S.R., and China. But both sides built and stored huge numbers of atomic and other weapons. Military threats and political tension were in the news every week. Each side supported different countries in political and military battles around the world, including Asia, Africa, Latin America, and the Caribbean, even when these battles had little to do with communism or democracy.

The United States shaped much of its immigration policy to help refugees from communist countries. It also aided refugees to remind the world that America was a country of freedom, not racism. The government passed laws to accept people who were no longer living in their home countries because political boundaries had changed, or who would be persecuted if they returned home after World War II. These immigrants would not be counted in the quota system. The Displaced Persons Act of 1948—extended for two more years in 1950—admitted 415,000 refugees to the United States over four years. The law applied only

These Hungarian refugees are walking through Yugoslavia on their way to shelter in March 1957, after their failed revolt against the Soviet Union.

to Europeans (not Asians) who had suffered hardships. Some were Jews who had been persecuted by the Nazis, but many others were allowed to immigrate because they were anti-communist.

Aniela Szeliga was a young woman who did not have to return to communist Poland. She was nineteen when she was taken by Nazi soldiers and forced to labor on a farm in Germany. After the war, she spent four years in a military facility run by the United States and its allies. She was admitted to the United States as a refugee in 1949. "For me, being in America the freedom was the thing: that you can go to church, you can speak, you can write, you can talk," Szeliga explained. "In Poland, people from the cities didn't respect ordinary people from the country. . . . I found it's not like that over here; you can go to your priest, shake hands, talk freely like I talk to you or anyone. But in Poland you couldn't, and it was a free Poland when I grew up. But there's freedom—and then there's real freedom. . . . Several years ago, I went back to Poland [and] . . . my sister said to me, 'Aren't you sad to go back to America?' I said, 'No, I'm not sad. I know I was born here . . . but America is my country now.'"

After a failed revolt by Hungarians against the Soviet Union in 1956, 35,000 Hungarians came as refugees to the United States. "I was in my second year of high school," recalled Ava Rado-Harte.

That night . . . the Russians came in with tanks . . . and there was a lot of fighting. . . . Many people were shot dead on the street. . . . I wasn't allowed to go out. . . . My [family] . . . arranged for a guide to help us escape. We took a train to a . . . city near the Austrian border. . . . We had to take another small train to a small village. . . . [The] Russian guards were there . . . with questions, so our guide had us go to the back of the train and then under the train in the dark to nearby houses. . . . We were hiding and walking in the dark through the gardens and gates until we got to this forest on the border. We were still in Hungary. The Russians set flares to catch the escapees. . . . Each time a flare went up, we hit the ground so they wouldn't see us, and the only thing we had was the clothes on our backs. . . . [Our guide] finally took us to the first place that had a light on when we crossed the border.

Rado-Harte waited with other refugees to be flown out of Munich, Germany. "They played the American and Hungarian national anthems as we were getting on the airplane," she remembered.

In the early 1960s, Cubans like Alejandro began coming in large numbers. In 1965, when Fidel Castro said that Cubans with relatives who had emigrated were free to leave, President Lyndon Johnson "declare[d] . . . to the people of Cuba that those who seek refuge here in America will find it. . . . [Our tradition] as an asylum for the oppressed is going to be upheld." This was an open invitation. Many of the first wave of Cubans who came to the United States believed the communist government would fall and they could return to Cuba. Many Americans believed this, too. Yet this has not happened and there have been several waves of immigration. In 2015, however, President Barack Obama opened up diplomatic relations with Cuba, beginning a new era.

One of the most famous immigration waves from Cuba lasted from April 15 to September 26, 1980. Castro again announced that Cubans who wanted to emigrate could leave. They crowded the port of Mariel and sailed out in makeshift boats. This became known as "the Mariel Boatlift." About 125,000 Cubans made it into the United States. Castro had sent some criminals from Cuban prisons as well, upsetting Americans. In 1984, a number of Cubans were returned to their country, but most stayed here as refugees. In 1995, the United States and Cuba reached an agreement that no fewer than 20,000 legal U.S. visas would be given to Cubans each year. Those trying to reach America illegally by boat were sent

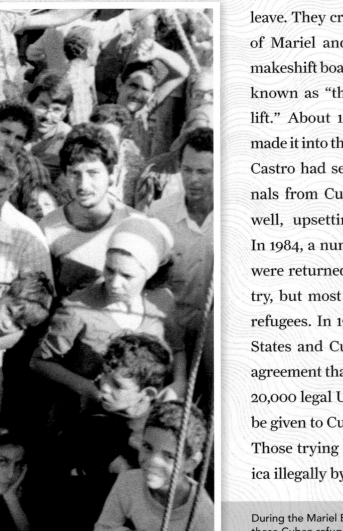

During the Mariel Boatlift of 1980, these Cuban refugees landed at Key West, Florida.

back to Cuba if they were captured at sea by the U.S. Coast Guard. But if they landed in the United States, they were usually accepted as political refugees.

"To me, the decision to come to America was not about money," said Emilio Estefan, who immigrated to the United States from Cuba when he was fifteen. He became a famous record producer. "I always looked at the United States as a place that represented freedom, that you have the right to free expression, have the right to any dream. But to me, more than anything else as a kid, I was afraid to live in a Communist country.... When we used to have dinner or lunch, we had to talk quietly because [my mom and dad] were afraid somebody was listening to them. So my whole motivation was really fear—fear that I should live in a country where I am afraid to talk or have an opinion."

Cold War politics produced another large group of refugees: South Vietnamese. Fighting in Vietnam started after World War II. The Vietnamese people sought to gain independence from France. This was achieved in 1954, but the country was split into North Vietnam and South Vietnam. Troops from North Vietnam, which was communist, continued to battle South Vietnam (whose government was friendly to the United States), wanting to rule Vietnam as one country. The United States supported the South Vietnamese and, by the early 1960s, was sending American soldiers to what became known as the Vietnam War. Although peace agreements were signed in 1973 (by then most Americans had withdrawn), fighting continued until 1975, when the communists were victorious.

South Vietnamese who had helped the Americans—from political leaders to ordinary people—were terrified to stay in their country. The United States evacuated many prominent supporters in emergency rescue operations. "On April 28, 1975, my extended family group was driven to Tan Son Nhut Air Base," recounted Trong Nguyen, who had been an officer in the South Vietnamese army and worked for an American aid organization. "There was a large crowd of maybe ten thousand people waiting at the terminal.... We kept the kids close to us.... Around 5:00 A.M., C-46 helicopters landed in front of us.... People hurried to the helicopters. My own family was divided onto three different aircraft. We landed on the huge boat, the *Pioneer Contender*. I had mixed emotions. I felt that we were going to heaven—the United States. But I already missed my country. I realized that I would never see Vietnam again."

The family settled in Chicago, where they were first met with hostility. "When I worked as a janitor . . . a co-worker told me, 'Trong, do you know that America is overpopulated? We have more than two hundred million people. We don't need you. Go back where you belong.' I was shocked to hear people trying to

Within ten years, however, the Vietnamese community grew. What had once been a slum area of Chicago had "more than fifty Vietnamese family-owned businesses. . . . There are also stores owned by Khmer [Cambodians], Lao, Chinese, Ethiopians, a Jewish kosher butcher, two Hispanic grocers, a black record shop, and an American bar. There are Japanese, Thai, Indian, and Mexican restaurants. . . . And a McDonald's." The early-1980s neighborhood Trong Nguyen described is the melting pot that Americans see themselves as being.

After the first wave, South Vietnamese continued to flee.

chase us out. I thought, 'Who is going to feed the children?'" Trong's wife, Thanh, defended herself to co-workers in a factory: "'Vietnam is a small country, but we did not come to America to look for jobs. We're political refugees. We can't go back home.'"

In 1978 and 1979, they began leaving secretly in boats, many of which were dangerous to travel in. These refugees came to be known as the Vietnamese boat people. The term included Cambodians and Laotians who had been involved in the Vietnam War and also Chinese

Before they were able to come to the United States, many Vietnamese lived first in refugee camps in other Asian countries. This group is from the Songkhla camp in Thailand, where 5,800 refugees were sheltering in July 1979.

who felt persecuted in communist Vietnam. Boat people continued to leave into the 1990s. The United Nations records that about one-third died at sea, from storms, starvation, and attacks by pirates. More than a million lived in refugee camps in Southeast Asia and the Pacific Islands, some for many years.

Tuan Nguyen (not related to Trong Nguyen) paid seven bars of gold so his family could leave Vietnam on a small boat with 120 other refugees in 1989. He and his wife had three children. "We didn't know if anyone would pick us up or if they'd send us back to Vietnam or if we'd die on the ocean," he said.

They spent sixteen years in a refugee camp in the Philippines. He had no rights as a citizen and worked thirteen hours a day selling perfume and soap from door to door. In 2005, the United States finally agreed to accept him and his family. It had been his dream, but when he arrived in California he said, "It's not a dream for me. It's for my children—to grow up here, to get an education and to become the best citizens they can be. That is my goal: to give them a better life."

In 1979, the Islamic Revolution toppled the nonreligious but nondemocratic government in Iran. The United States had supported this government and accepted some Iranian refugees—many wealthy, or middle-class, educated, and professional—into the United States. An Iranian girl named Roya immigrated to the United States in the early 1980s with her parents. "They came seeking a country with civil liberties and better economic opportunities," she recalled. The family kept practicing its Islamic faith. "I really didn't have issues with 'fitting in' on the outside," said Roya. "I didn't have a noticeable accent and didn't look or dress much differently than most American kids. On the inside, however, I never felt like I fit in anywhere until I made little safe spaces for myself."

Just like many immigrants before her, refugees like Roya experienced prejudice. "I have been rejected for different reasons, the worst one being ignorance about who I am by teachers and classmates. I now realize there are all kinds of people and you should look for the most understanding ones whenever possible. . . . I . . . would like Americans to know that I didn't have an oil well in my backyard and I didn't ride a camel to school, even though I saw a lot of camel caravans. . . . Camels are *very* cool!"

These children, whose heritage is Albanian, lived in plastic shelters in 1998 in the hills near Kosovo. Kosovo, which declared its independence in 2008, had been part of Yugoslavia until that country broke up in the 1990s.

The United States frequently changes policies about different groups of political refugees, especially in an emergency. After a war or genocide—such as Jewish people experienced during World War II—Congress can pass laws or the president can change rules to allow people from a specific country to come here. In the early 1990s, as the country of Yugoslavia was breaking up, war broke out between different ethnic groups trying to establish independence. The United States accepted 131,000 refugees from what became Bosnia. In 1999, it allowed 20,000 refugees from Kosovo, under attack from the Serbian government that ruled them, to come to America. "In 1998, when I was about 17 years old . . . nearby towns and villages were bombed," recalled a young man named Fatim from Kosovo. Fatim is an ethnic Albanian and a Muslim. "With [Serbian] . . . soldiers pointing guns at us, my family walked out of our house. There already were about 3,000 people walking down the road. . . . When I looked back, I could see that our house was already on fire. . . . One of my relatives was shot." Fatim and his family made it to a refugee camp in Macedonia and eventually to the United States. Now married and a father, he helps new refugees who come to America.

Some Americans are not happy with refugees in their communities. In the 1970s, when South Vietnamese refugees were coming to the United States, Robert Gnaizda of the California Health and Welfare Agency predicted, "If we get a small number, we are going to take care of them. . . . [But] no American would welcome Vietnamese if in fact they are going to disrupt the economy and the housing market." A Gallup Poll in 1975 found that 54 percent of Americans were opposed to taking in Vietnamese refugees, and only 36 percent in favor.

Half of the people living in Clarkston, Georgia, in 2007 were refugees. They began to be placed there by resettlement agencies in the late 1980s. By 2007, the high school had students from more than fifty countries. Yet Clarkston's mayor, Lee Swaney, forbade anyone from playing soccer in the town park. "There will be nothing but baseball down here as long as I am mayor," he said. "Those fields weren't made for soccer." To Swaney, baseball was an American game and soccer was not, and the refugees were not welcome.

Many Americans do, however, believe we should accept refugees. Church groups and nonprofit agencies are active in helping them. "Refugees, many of whom arrive having lost everything, become some of the most resilient . . . and devoted citizens we have," wrote Senator John Kerry in 2010. (He went on to become Secretary of State.) "The difference between these individuals, and so many sitting in refugee camps, is that a new country [the United States] took a chance on them."

"By protecting refugees from persecution, we honor our nation's finest traditions," said Senator Edward "Ted" Kennedy of Massachusetts. Throughout his time in Congress, Kennedy championed legislation to help refugees come to the United States.

Even when Americans welcome them, it has not been easy for immigrants to prove that they are refugees in danger, rather than people trying to come to the United States for economic reasons. (Remember, the vast majority of nineteenth- and early-twentieth-century immigrants whose descendants are American citizens did come for economic opportunity.) During the 1980s and 1990s, civil war and violations of civil rights in Central American countries, including Nicaragua, Guatemala, and El Salvador, brought many people seeking asylum to the United States. "I was in jail for 32 months," said a young Salvadorian woman named Carmen in an interview in 1984. "I was jailed with no charges at all, and I was not allowed to have a lawyer for defense. I think that is against my human rights." Yet many political refugees like Carmen were not given permission to stay in the United States because the U.S. government decided that they came for economic opportunity. It did not believe that they faced prison or death if they returned to their home countries.

However, in 1997, Congress passed the Nicaraguan Adjustment and Central American Relief Act, allowing those who had escaped these countries and who had come without documents to the United States to apply for permanent residence. They had to have lived here for at least five years. This law also covered refugees who fled eastern European countries that had been under the control of the former Soviet Union until the early 1990s.

The Haitian Refugee Immigration Fairness Act of 1998 offered Haitians the same opportunities to apply for permission to stay in the United States legally. Haitians had been fleeing dictatorship and poverty since the early 1970s, but most were returned by the U.S. government to their country. In September 1991, a military coup replaced the democratic government. Within six months, 38,000 Haitians had been stopped trying to flee by boat. About 10,000 were allowed to apply for refuge in the United States. As they waited for the decision on whether they would be accepted as refugees, thousands lived in camps at the American military base at Guantánamo, Cuba. Many were not accepted. In 1994, a democratic government was restored and Haitian emigration slowed. But many Haitians continued to come in the 2000s, some without documents. After a devastating earthquake in Haiti in 2010, President Barack Obama allowed undocumented Haitians living in the United States to have work visas but did not take them in as refugees.

When she was six years old, in 1994, Clemantine Wamariya left her home in Rwanda with her sixteen-year-old sister. They fled ethnic genocide. "I did not know at that age what a genocide was," said Wamariya, "or what it meant to kill another person. I grew up with all my neighbors [of various ethnic groups] as friends." With the first outbreak of violence, they took shelter in their grandparents' house, but it was attacked. The girls hid in a field. "We were hiding for a very long time, thinking that the screaming and shooting would stop. But it didn't stop, so . . . we just kept going, crawling for days and days."

For six years the sisters lived in refugee camps in various African countries. They were allowed to enter the United States in 2000. In 2006, Clemantine won an essay con-test sponsored by talk-show host Oprah Winfrey and went on to study at Yale University. She has been back to Rwanda to help others.

Wars, genocide, natural disasters like famine, and the need for refuge have continued into the twenty-first century. In 2004, Congress passed the North Korean Human Rights Act to grant political refuge to North Koreans. The United States had fought on the side of South Korea in the Korean War (1950–53), which ended with the division of Korea into two countries, North and South Korea. However, Koreans at the time did not immigrate

Refugees from ethnic genocide—the killing of an entire group of people by another—fled Rwanda, often spending years in camps in other parts of Africa. These children are at a United Nations camp in Goma, Zaire (now the Democratic Republic of the Congo), in 1994. Some Rwandan refugees were eventually accepted by the United States. Others were not.

in large numbers to America. North Koreans took refuge in South Korea and in other Asian countries. But severe famine, which started in 1994, and the brutal repression of human rights, led to passage of the 2004 law. By 2011, only 122 North Korean refugees had come to this country. One of them was Joseph Kim, who immigrated when he was seventeen. His father had died of starvation, and his mother and sister disappeared trying to escape to China. At fifteen years old, he fled to China and was helped by a humanitarian organization to come to the United States.

"I had to do anything to survive," said Kim, who swam across a river to get to China. "I just didn't understand why it was happening to me. I couldn't even blame it on someone else. . . . [In] North Korea there's nothing I could blame or ask. I couldn't find answers." Kim was placed in a foster home in Virginia with children from Myanmar. "My dream . . . is to go to college," he said. "I like to play soccer a lot. Some say my hobby is studying but that is not true. I like to eat. I like to hang out with friends." In 2013, Kim told a reporter, "I did not come here by myself. I had hope, but hope by itself is not enough, many people helped me along the way. . . . This is my message to you. Have hope for yourself but also help each other. Life can be hard for everyone, wherever you live. . . . [You] may . . . change someone's life with even the smallest act of love."

The September 11, 2001, terrorist destruction of the World Trade Center in New York and part of the Pentagon in Washington, D.C., led to two wars: one in Afghanistan, which started in October 2001, and one in Iraq, begun in 2003. The reasons for both wars were politically complex, but for many Americans, the goal was to bring Islamic terrorists to justice and prevent more terrorist attacks. Some of the Iraqi and Afghan people who supported the United States in these wars came as refugees to the United States.

However, from 2003 to January 2007, the United States had accepted only about 450 political refugees from Iraq. Some Americans realized how unfair this was to people who had helped the United States. In 2008, after military personnel who had served in Iraq and the media protested against the small numbers, many more began to be accepted; the total reached about 100,000 in 2013. One of these was a man named Adil Ibrahim, who had been an interpreter for the American military.

"I never thought I'd leave Iraq," he said. "I thought it was home. But after the events of 2005 to 2007, these events were telling me I needed to leave. My friends were getting killed, getting kidnapped, it [was] becoming hard to live your life." In 2006, Ibrahim's father had been kidnapped, and although he paid a ransom, his father was never returned.

Civil war in Afghanistan, and the American war against terrorism there, destroyed many parts of the country. In 2002, these Afghans pass in front of ruined buildings in Kabul, Afghanistan's capital.

With a wife, stepdaughter, and son, he felt, "It was difficult for me to stay there and see that there would be a future for me and my family." He now serves in the American military.

The United Nations counts more than 55,000 Afghan refugees who have been accepted in the United States between 2002 and 2012. The numbers started going down in 2007, when only about 2,300 Afghan refugees were admitted.

Civil war in Syria (fighting began in 2011) created more than 2 million refugees by July 2014. Almost all of them live in camps in nearby countries, including Jordan, Lebanon, and Turkey. The United States took about 1,400 refugees from Syria in 2012. By early January 2014, some 135,000 Syrians had applied for refuge in the United States and were waiting to hear if they would be accepted.

The United States does help refugees in other ways. By 2014, the country had sent more than $1 billion to help Syrians with humanitarian (nonmilitary) aid. But it is still difficult to enter the United States as a refugee, especially since the terrorist attacks on September 11, 2001. Americans continue to worry about immigrants who practice Islam, since Islamic militant terrorist attacks continue around the world. In 2003, the U.S. Citizenship and Immigration Services was placed under the new Department of Homeland Security formed after the attacks. Many of the rules are designed to keep out terrorists, but how many refugees who are not terrorists do they then keep out?

Americans might think about the words of Rwandan refugee Clemantine Wamariya: "There are so many people who have lost their families through wars and genocide and hunger. I'm really grateful for my life. I've realized that there is a way that life can be simple, that

you can be thankful for the hot water, for the streets you walk on, for the rights that you have and for having parents."

"Welcoming and accepting refugees whose lives have been robbed from them is so important," she added in a blog post in 2013. "Refugees are going to be the next generation of leaders who shape the United States, their own countries of origin and beyond. We, more than anybody else, understand the value of peace, and are going to be leaders that promote it."

Refugees from civil war in Syria have continued to live in neighboring countries. This 2012 photo shows some of the tens of thousands of tents at the Za'atari camp in Jordan. The United States started accepting larger numbers of Syrian refugees in 2014.

THIS LAND IS WHOSE LAND?

FROM WORLD WAR II INTO THE TWENTY-FIRST CENTURY

"I didn't want to stay in one place. It was always my desire for adventure and the place I really wanted to visit was the U.S. There is so much opportunity with all the modern facilities and technology," explained Perla Rabor Rigor, who came to the United States from the Philippines as part of an exchange program for international study begun in 1948 with the Information and Educational Exchange Act. Already a registered nurse, she worked in American hospitals and stayed in this country for the rest of her life.

"It was a rough time for me when I started here," she said, "because being from a foreign land you have to push yourself to get your ability recognized." By 1975, she had earned degrees in psychology and education. "To me . . . success is not measured by the position the person has reached in life, but by the obstacles she or he has overcome."

During World War II, American policies and attitudes about refugees began to change. Laws regarding refugees continue to be modified in the twenty-first century. In this same period—from about 1940 through 2015—laws concerning other kinds of immigrants have also changed. Since China was an American ally in World War II, as early as 1943, Congress repealed all Chinese exclusion laws. The law also stated that Chinese (but not other Asian peoples) could become American citizens.

In 1946, when the Philippines became independent, Filipinos were allowed to become American citizens, too, as were people born in India. The annual immigration quota for Chinese was set at only 105 people, however, and at 100 for Filipinos. The small quotas for Asian groups indicated that racism was still a factor in immigration policy. But allowing Asians to become citizens meant that they could bring in family members outside the quota system. And educational/work exchanges like the one that brought Perla Rigor from the Philippines provided another path to becoming an American without being counted in national quotas.

In the late 1940s and early 1950s, Americans were again debating who should be allowed to immigrate to the United States. "I believe that this nation is the last hope of Western civilization and if this oasis of the world shall be over-run, perverted, contaminated or destroyed, then the last flickering light of humanity will be extinguished," proclaimed Senator Patrick McCarran of Nevada. "I take no issue with those who would praise the contributions which have been made to our society by people of many races, of varied creeds and colors. . . . However, we have in the United States today hard-core, indigestible blocs which have not become integrated into the American way of life, but which, on the contrary are its deadly enemies. Today, as never before, untold millions are storming our gates for admission and those gates are cracking under the strain."

In 1952, the McCarran-Walter Act temporarily settled the debate in favor of keeping national quotas. President Harry Truman vetoed the act, saying, "The basis of this quota system was false and unworthy in 1924. It is even worse now. At the present time, this quota system keeps out the very people we want to bring in. It is incredible to me that, in this year of 1952, we should again be enacting into law such a slur on the patriotism, the capacity, and the decency of a large part of our citizenry." Congress overrode his veto.

The law made some small changes to the 1924 quota laws: it based quota numbers on the 1920 census. Great Britain, Germany, and the Republic of Ireland received two-thirds of the quota slots. Each country in Asia had a quota of 100 people per year, and no more than 2,000 immigrants from all of Asia could come in each year. It also placed quotas on the number of immigrants from European colonies in the Western Hemisphere, mostly in the Caribbean, including Jamaica and Barbados, which at that time were still colonies of Great Britain. Other countries in the Western Hemisphere, such as Mexico, continued to have no quotas. Up to 50 percent of each quota was saved for highly skilled immigrants and their families. The law also favored parents, husbands or wives, and children of American citizens.

The well-known chef Jacques Pépin immigrated to the United States when he was twenty-three under this quota system.

By 1959, I wanted to come to America. Everyone wanted to come to America! ... They accepted only so many immigrants from different countries every year, and the quota for France was never filled, as opposed to, say, Italy, where ... there was a huge waiting list going back eight, ten years before you could come to the United States with an immigrant visa, but France? No. ... I had my green card [the document that allows an immigrant to stay permanently in the United States] in three months. ... I came here on the tenth of September 1959, and a couple of days later I was working at Le Pavillon, which was the best restaurant in the country at the time.

Pépin added, "I would never move back to France because I'm much more American than French now. ... After fifty years here, I've become totally American."

But the McCarran-Walter Act also did something that would dramatically change immigration: it took away the barriers for Asians to become citizens of the United States. Americans at the time did not think this would have much impact on our country; the quota numbers for Asian countries were small. But as Asians already living in the United States became citizens, they could bring in husbands or wives and children outside of the quota numbers.

Laws don't always have the consequences

Patricia Violante holds her mother Agata's hand as they board a ship in 1956 in Naples, Italy, to make their home in the United States. Her father, Renato, leads the family. Patricia was five years old when they sailed, settling in Washington, D.C.

that Congress intends. They also don't reflect the actual number of immigrants that come each year. The 1952 immigration law was in effect for thirteen years; the quota provided for about 2 million immigrants in this period. In fact, some 3.5 million people immigrated legally to the United States, including Latinos, Canadians, refugees, and immediate family not affected by the law. In 1953, 8,000 Asian immigrants entered; by 1965, the total number of Asian immigrants was 236,000.

Diana Yu was twenty-one when she emigrated from Korea to attend college in Alabama. She raised her three daughters while attending graduate school in the United States. "In America I learned to do things myself, solve my own problems instead [of] expecting someone else to solve it for me," she said. "I owe a lot to America. It has been my training ground. This country has taught me some of the most important lessons in life. Moreover, I like living in a multicultural/multiracial society."

Once some of the racial barriers for Asians had been removed, many immigrants from China and Korea came to attend American colleges in the 1950s and 1960s. They were highly educated and skilled. By 2010, Asians were immigrating to the United States in higher numbers than Hispanics who entered legally. In 2013, Asian Americans were the fastest-growing group descended from immigrants in the United States.

Although racial barriers persisted, by the early 1960s the modern civil rights movement to gain equal treatment for African Americans was under way. Many Americans were embarrassed by the difference between our ideals as a free country and the reality of segregation. This was true of immigration laws, too. Americans realized that setting different limits for immigrants coming from different countries—usually favoring people from western and northern Europe—was a form of discrimination. Large majorities in both houses of Congress passed the Immigration and Nationality Act of 1965 (the Hart-Celler Act). It was signed into law by President Lyndon Johnson at the Statue of Liberty. The law eliminated all national quotas; from then on, it would not matter what country a potential immigrant came from.

But the 1965 law did set quotas for the Eastern and Western Hemispheres. The Eastern Hemisphere includes Europe, Asia, Africa, and Australia; its quota was set at 170,000 immigrants a year. The Western Hemisphere, including North, Central, and South America as well as the Caribbean, had a quota of 120,000. This was the first time a limit had been set on immigrants from the Americas. In 1976, the hemisphere quotas were eliminated—290,000 immigrants from anywhere in the world could enter the United States each year.

President Lyndon Johnson signs the 1965 immigration reform bill into law at the Statue of Liberty, with New York City in the background. The law eliminated country quotas that had been established in the 1920s.

Race and employment, however, were still two big fears. To pass the law, supporters had to convince Americans that it would not change the ethnic character of the United States or overwhelm America with immigrants. Senator Ted Kennedy of Massachusetts predicted the law "will not flood our cities with immigrants. It will not upset the ethnic mix of society. . . . It will not cause American workers to lose their jobs."

"It is obvious . . . that the great days of immigration have long since run their course," said Sidney Yates, a congressman from Illinois, who believed that millions of people would no longer come to this country.

Were they right? In the 1950s, there were about 250,000 legal immigrants a year to this country. Within forty years, there would be more than four times as many coming to the United States. Just as in the past, immigrants were looking for ways to make a living and improve their children's lives in a world that is often politically and economically unstable. By the 1980s, more than 80 percent of documented immigrants came from Asia and Latin America. It is impossible to tell how many undocumented immigrants come—not only from Latin America but from all over the

Paterson, New Jersey, hosts a growing population of Islamic immigrants, including these young women eating a nighttime meal during the month of Ramadan, in 2006.

world. Europeans, Canadians, Asians, and others stay on after their visitor or tourist visas expire. One estimate puts the number of illegal immigrants at 12 million people between 2000 and 2010.

The number of African immigrants grew after the 1965 immigration law passed. Tunde Ayobami came here from Nigeria when he was twenty-one, in 1969. At first, he lived in Rhode Island. "I was the first Nigerian in the area. Before I came here, none of us had the idea of going to the suburbs. . . . But I tell them this place is really peaceful. . . . I try to find jobs for them and find school at the same time." Ayobami got a degree in medical technology. He wanted to sell technical equipment. "Most people didn't think I could make it. First, because of my [Nigerian] accent, they said I would never sell [to] anybody." But he got the job. "Since I've been on the road," he said, "my territory has been improved about 200 percent." He has encountered prejudice in the United States, but he explained, "I became understanding. People are this way, they're not going to change; I'm going to change. I became tolerant."

Immigrants also came from the Middle East. E. Murat Tuzcu emigrated from Turkey in 1985. He was already a medical doctor and received a visa for physician training. "I spoke good English, but I did not know many of the standardized ways of doing things in U.S. hos-pitals. I was working twelve-, fourteen-hour days," he said. Because his visa was a temporary one, to stay in the United States permanently, Dr. Tuzcu had to work in a part of the country that did not have enough doctors. He worked at a Veterans Administration hospital in Pittsburgh and received his green card.

The Dos Reis family emigrated from Brazil in 1992. In 2003, they became American citizens at a ceremony in Hyde Park, New York. Standing in front of a statue of President Franklin Roosevelt are Renata Dos Reis and her three sons (left to right): Matheus, Isaac, and Orlando. Their father, Roberto, is the photographer. Matheus and Orlando became citizens when their parents did. Isaac, who was born in Florida, was an American citizen by birth.

Now he is a noted cardiologist and teacher at the Cleveland Clinic in Ohio. "I feel as much a part of this country as I do a part of Turkey," he said. "I don't think that I have to choose to be Turkish or an American. I really think that I can be both."

The path to legal immigration keeps changing, as do the laws. The American economy suffered recessions beginning in 1975, raising fears once again that immigrants would take jobs from American citizens. In 1978, Congress created the Select Commission on Immigration and Refugee Policy to come up with solutions. Father Theodore Hesburgh, who had been president of Notre Dame University, headed the commission. Father Hesburgh wrote in the *New York Times* in 1986, "During the next 15 years, assuming a persistently strong economy, the United States will create about 30 million new jobs. Can we afford to set aside more than 20 percent of them for foreign workers? No. It would be a disservice to our own poor and unfortunate."

But the commission did propose that undocumented immigrants who had been in the United States for a long time be granted legal status. It also recommended stricter border patrols to keep new people out. The two recommendations were meant to balance each other by controlling immigration growth.

The Immigration Reform and Control Act of 1986, signed into law by President Ronald Reagan, followed these suggestions. It allowed longtime undocumented immigrants to apply to be legal residents and eventually citizens. It increased the number of border patrols. It also set penalties for Americans who knowingly hired illegal immigrants. But fining American employers was a controversial provision and difficult to enforce without seeming to violate Americans' rights. Although border security increased, undocumented Mexicans and others continued to cross into the United States; they found other routes to get here. By 1998, an estimated 2.68 million illegal immigrants had become permanent residents. This was 88 percent of all those who had applied.

In 1990, the Immigration and Nationality Act allowed a total of 700,000 immigrants to come to the United States each year. The easiest way to enter was as the family member of someone who was already here; the law also allowed more people to immigrate for work.

Golly Ramnath, an Asian Indian who lived in Trinidad, was forty-one when she came to the United States in 1998. For five years she worked as a live-in babysitter in Connecticut under a visa that made her return to Trinidad every six months. In 2002, she started studying for a high school degree. "In my culture, the girls are not pushed for an education," she said. "You're pushed, really, to take care of the house and your family, and that's it. . . . You know how to read and write, but you have to cook, clean the house, learn to sew, and take care of your husband and your children. . . . I came to America to find a better life, but I realized that to have a good life here, you need to be educated or else you're stuck in a menial job." She graduated from Brooklyn College in 2009. "I was fifty-two years old! . . . You cannot give in to the stumbling blocks that will come into your life. . . . People say this country is the land flowing with milk and honey, but you don't see that milk and honey until you work for it."

Many, many immigrant stories start with difficulty, involve hard work, and end with success. This is as true now as it was for the first European colonists. Kiril Tarpov emigrated from Bulgaria in 2000. "I received an invitation from the Bulgarian Eastern Orthodox Church based in New York to become their music conductor, and they offered me a work visa. . . . I came here . . . to have a future as a musician, and second, to give a chance to my adopted son because he has dark skin—his parents were Egyptian, and back in Bulgaria we have a lot of problems with people with dark skin color." He found less racism in the United States.

This Latino family has just crossed the Rio Bravo River near the Mexican city of Juarez, as they try to enter the United States in 2006.

To make more money, Tarpov took a job at a coffee shop. "I didn't speak any English. But I was working with the customers, and it's amazing how kind they were. They took their time to explain things to me, what things meant, like 'bagel with cream cheese.' . . . Some of them came just to help me and teach me. . . . That's why I respect and love New Yorkers."

The support of Americans has been essential to enabling immigrants to assimilate and thrive. Church groups and pro-immigrant organizations often help individual immigrants or generally fight for immigrant rights.

Kiril Tarpov came legally to the United States. Carlos Escobar came illegally from Mexico in 1996. "I had been a . . . construction worker, but the company I worked for closed. . . . I wanted my son to have a good education and maybe one day go to college, which was never a possibility for me. . . . When I was little, I sold food on the street so my family could eat." He paid a coyote $3,000 to get him across the U.S. border. "At one point we didn't have a drink of water for nearly two days. . . . There were lots of rattlesnakes, scorpions, heat, dust. . . . I could see the lights of the American Border Patrol. . . . The coyote told us that many like us did not make it."

One way for legal immigrants to become American citizens is to serve in the U.S. military. These members of the military were among those naturalized in 2010 in a ceremony in San Antonio, Texas. They came from Panama, Kuwait, Nigeria, Belarus, Turkey, and the Philippines.

But Escobar succeeded. He worked long days in a vineyard in northern California. He studied English in a class held in the basement of a church at night. With help from his English teacher, he was finally able to get a green card and, after seven years, brought his wife and son to the United States. "This was the greatest day of my life," he said. Eventually, he became an American citizen. His son went to college; he wants to be a lawyer who helps other immigrants.

Should immigrants who enter without documents, like Carlos Escobar, be allowed to get green cards or become American citizens? This is one of the biggest issues in the debate about immigration today. Some Americans think it would be sensible and fair, especially if the immigrants have lived here for years, worked, and paid taxes. Others think it would be rewarding people who broke the law—they see illegal immigrants as criminals.

The one thing all Americans seem to agree on is that we have to reform our immigration laws. But they cannot agree on how to reform them. Republicans in Congress and state offices tend to favor no amnesty for illegals and stricter controls for entry. ("Amnesty" means the United States would ignore the fact that immigrants came without documents and provide a path to stay permanently or become citizens.) Democrats often support amnesty and would allow larger numbers of immigrants in, but they also want to strengthen controls. Politics play an important role in their attitudes. Legal immigrants who become citizens are voters, and politicians and lawmakers don't want to lose their votes. But they don't want to lose the anti-immigrant vote, either. The American public seems to be as divided as the government on what should happen about immigration law reform. As of mid-2015, no comprehensive immigration reform law had been passed.

It takes a lot of paperwork and a lot of time (often years) to process legal immigration applications. Pro-immigration Americans argue that there would be fewer illegal immigrants if it were easier to apply for the needed documents. They want to simplify the process.

Americans both for and against increased immigration seem to agree that the United States should welcome immigrants to fill jobs that require special education and training. And many employers want workers to fill unskilled jobs. But are there enough American workers already who can fill these jobs? Some people argue that Americans are not willing to do low-paying jobs, like cleaning and janitorial work, that immigrants are willing to do.

Perhaps the most newsworthy question is: How can we keep immigrants from crossing illegally over the border with Mexico? In 2010, 58 percent of undocumented immigrants were Mexican (about 6.5 million people), and 23 percent came through Mexico from other parts of Latin America. About 11 percent (1.3 million) of undocumented immigrants were from Asia; 4 percent from Europe and Canada; and 3 percent from Africa and other countries. Illegal immigrants cross the border with Canada as well. In 2010, nearly 7,500 people were caught trying to cross from Canada. The countries they came from included Albania, the Czech Republic, Israel, and India. Many cross by boat or Jet Ski, or by swimming to states like Michigan, New York, and Minnesota. In 2011, more suspected terrorists were caught trying to enter the United States through Canada than through Mexico, according to the U.S. Customs and Border Protection Agency. Yet most Americans are far more concerned with undocumented Latin American immigrants than with those from other countries.

Some Americans have been concerned that illegal immigrants and their children receive government health and social services and free public education. American citizens pay for these benefits through taxes. But illegal immigrants also pay taxes. They pay sales, gasoline, and property taxes, and studies show that they also pay federal and state income taxes and Social Security taxes. Yet in 1994, Californians voted in favor of Proposition 187, which said that illegal immigrants could not have these benefits of being an American citizen. (California withdrew the law in 1999.)

The 1996 platform of the Republican Party included these words: "We support a constitutional amendment . . . declaring that children born in the United States of parents who are not legally present in the United States or who are not long-term residents are not automatically citizens." In 1996, Congress passed

This photo shows part of the fence that separates the United States and Mexico, built when Congress passed the Secure Fence Act in 2006. The fence has not been completed.

a law reducing the number of public benefits to legal immigrants if they were not citizens of the United States.

Fears of illegal immigrants continued to grow after 2000, leading Congress to pass the Secure Fence Act of 2006. This law called for building physical barriers, including high fences, along the border with Mexico. Mexico and other Latin American countries were offended by the idea of an actual fence separating the United States from these countries. The law was controversial, and it was hard to prove how effective it was in keeping undocumented immigrants out. Building the barriers was expensive, and in some places mountains and water patterns make it difficult to construct; as of 2015, the fence had not been completed.

Although the federal government is in charge of immigration, states with large Latino immigrant populations sometimes pass their own laws. In 2010, Arizona passed law SB 1070 against illegal immigrants. The law made it possible for police to arrest suspected undocumented immigrants without getting a warrant from a judge. It became a state crime not to carry official government identification papers, and illegal immigrants could not try to get work in the United States. The federal government immediately challenged the law. In 2012, the Supreme Court ruled against these three provisions. But the Supreme Court said that a fourth provision was legal: Arizona police could check whether a person was illegally in the United States if he or she were caught breaking any law—including traffic violations—if they had a "reasonable suspicion" that the person was undocumented. But what was "reasonable"? In many cases, it came down to whether the person looked Mexican. This is called "racial profiling."

Alabama, Georgia, Indiana, South Carolina, and Utah passed laws similar to Arizona's. They called for racial profiling, denying the opportunity to work or attend school, and other restrictions. After the Supreme Court's decision, these laws were being contested. However, other states, including New York, allow undocumented immigrants to have a driver's license or other form of identification. With some identification it is easier to live and work in the United States.

Perhaps the most important—and the most emotional—issue concerns the fate of children of illegal immigrants. In 2006, "[my] uncle was detained and deported [because] of the meatpacking plant raid that took place in Marshalltown [Iowa]," wrote a Mexican American teenager named Veronica. "My uncle's absence left a strong impact on my cousin, who was then 2, who stopped talking. . . . [My] aunt . . . was also eventually deported—regardless of having two citizen children, and having lived and worked in this country for over 15

Demonstrators in New York City in 2007 call for passage of the Dream Act. The Dream Act would allow young adults who were brought to the United States illegally as small children to remain in our country, the only home they remember.

years." The young children lived with Veronica's family for several years. In 2010, "[they] were reunited with their parents in Mexico. My cousin is now 9, and . . . feels alienated as he had never even visited the country [of Mexico]. . . . As citizens of the United States, it is truly a shame that both of these children are being denied their rights and benefits to have a brighter future as a result of our outdated and broken immigration laws."

Veronica's cousins were born in the United States and have the legal right to live here—

without their parents. Antonio Alarcón remembers illegally crossing the border with his parents when he was eleven. "Unfortunately, my little brother was too young to make the dangerous border crossing, so he stayed behind in Mexico with my grandparents. . . . I thought I would see him again soon, but I haven't seen him in nine years." In 2011, Alarcón's grandfather died; his grandmother died in

2012. "After my grandmother's death, my parents made the hardest decision of their life: they decided to return to Mexico to take care of my younger brother. Once again, my family was separated. My mother knew that I could have a better education and work opportunities in the U.S., so I decided to stay. It has been two years since I've seen my mom and dad. During these years, they have missed my high school graduation."

What happens to the children of illegal immigrants who were not born in the United States but were brought here when they were young? They have grown up as Americans, but they have no rights as citizens and are illegal. Should they be deported—sent back to their home countries? For years, Congress has considered a "Dream Act" that would grant young people like Antonio Alarcón the right to stay in the United States for a period of time. They could complete their education and become permanent legal residents or even citizens if they choose to. Some people argue this is only fair to children who did not make the decision to immigrate; others argue that letting them stay would reward the illegal behavior of their parents.

High school and college students have spoken out for the Dream Act. Pierre Berastaín's parents brought him from Peru to Texas when he was a child. He eventually graduated from Harvard and in 2012 was studying at Harvard Divinity School. "I am not a criminal, a monster . . . or someone who sits at home doing nothing," he said. "I care for this country. . . . I am not asking that our government maintain an open-door policy for immigrants. I am simply asking that it give an opportunity to those of us who have proven ourselves."

Not every child brought as an undocumented immigrant comes from Latin America. Manny Bartsch came to Ohio from Germany when he was seven, without the proper visa. He graduated from Heidelberg University in Ohio, but he still faced deportation from the United States. "I would go through any channel to correct this situation," he says. "I'm not asking for citizenship [but] I would love to earn it if that possibility would arise. . . . I would love to contribute to this country, give back to it. I just don't understand why they would educate people in my situation and deport them."

Al Okere's mother fled Nigeria after his father was killed because he had written an article that criticized the Nigerian government. Okere was five. His mother applied for refugee status but was refused and deported in 2005. Although his legal guardian is his aunt, an American citizen, Okere can still be forced to leave the United States. By 2012, he was a student at Central Washington University in Washington State, while the U.S. government was preparing to deport him. He believed, like many other illegal young adults, that he had been greatly aided by the people who knew him in America. "My family and community support has been enormous and it gives me zeal to work hard in my studies, to be able to lend a hand to others in need, to realize a bright future."

No national Dream Act had been passed by Congress by 2015. By the end of 2013, however, fifteen states had passed some form of the Dream Act, many offering help with college tuition in those states.

Many Americans—even those who worry about new immigration—support the idea of helping young immigrants who are already here. On August 15, 2012, President Barack Obama ordered that deportations of young illegals be stopped so that their situations could be evaluated. His program was called "Deferred Action for Childhood Arrivals" (DACA). The program could prevent many of them from having to return to countries that

About two million illegal immigrants were deported—sent back to their home countries—between 2008 and 2014. Here three young women protest against forced deportation in front of the U.S. Immigration and Customs Detention Center in Tacoma, Washington, in 2014. Undocumented children, as well as adults, can be deported.

are, in fact, foreign to them. It promises hope for people who view themselves as American in every way—they have gone to school here, they live in American communities—to continue to live as Americans.

Because the United States still provides hope for a better life, tens of thousands of Central American children illegally crossed the Mexican border in 2013 and 2014. They were sent by their parents—many of whom paid high prices to coyotes. The parents feared widespread violence in the countries these children came from, mainly Honduras, El Salvador, and Guatemala.

In 2013, more than one thousand people younger than twenty-three were killed in Honduras alone. "The first thing we can think of is to send our children to the United States," said a mother from San Pedro Sula in Honduras. "That's the idea, to leave."

"It's a serious social problem," added Elvin Flores, a police inspector in the neighborhood of La Pradera. "Any children born in this neighborhood are going to get involved in a gang."

The U.S. government kept most of these children in detention centers so that they could be deported. No one was happy. Republicans in Congress and state governments argued that because Democratic President Obama did not want to deport young people already here, Central American parents believed that the United States would not turn away these new children. Yet President Obama asked Congress to approve billions of dollars to improve security at the border and send most of the children home. Many Democrats disagreed with him and believed that the children should be allowed to stay as refugees. As of the autumn of 2014, the Obama administration had set up immigration offices in Central American countries to accept more children as refugees. U.S. officials were deciding, case by case, whether children without documents already in this country could stay if they faced danger at home.

In November 2014, President Obama declared that about 400,000 immigrants without documents would be allowed to stay in this country. They included undocumented parents of American citizens and young people who had been brought to the United States illegally by their parents before they were old enough to make their own decisions about where to live. But many Republicans in Congress and some Americans strongly objected. They believed it was Congress, not the president, that should make decisions about immigration, even though Congress has been unable to agree on a comprehensive immigration law. The debate about who should be able to immigrate to the United States and who can live here permanently continues as it has since the United States became a country more than two hundred years ago.

EPILOGUE

One could argue that people will always find a way to get into the United States if they want to badly enough. The aspirations and dreams that propel them are as strong as the resistance of those who would keep them out. Although some people see immigrants as taking jobs away from Americans or costing Americans money as they ask for social welfare, there is a long and well-documented history of the ways that immigrants have contributed to the United States. They have literally built this country from the ground up, and they continue to do so. They have overcome prejudice and thrived. Immigrants may not speak English, but their children and grandchildren do. The next generations often get better educations and better jobs. They serve in the American military. They hold government offices. They teach. Are they as American as those whose ancestors came before the United States was a country?

Am I an American? My great-grandparents came from Italy. They didn't speak much English. They lived in Italian neighborhoods in New York. They suffered from discrimination. They came in the 1880s and 1890s, when there was no limit on immigration. Had they tried to come after 1924, they almost certainly wouldn't have made it; there were fewer than 6,000 quota slots a year for Italians. They didn't have a lot of skills, although one of my great-grandfathers was a hatmaker; his wife, my great-grandmother, never learned to read or write. None of my great-grandparents were political refugees. Instead, they came for economic opportunity and a better life for their children and grandchildren and, as it turns out, for me. Would they be allowed to immigrate today?

Americans, in the past and in the present, answer the questions differently. But what can we all learn from the example of immigrants who persevered and prospered, even those from ethnic groups that suffered the most discrimination? Do we make it difficult, if not impossible, for new people to come? Do we deny them the rights of citizens? Do we treat them with fear and contempt? Or do we treat them as fellow human beings, with respect and compassion—the way we wish our immigrant ancestors had been treated, no matter who they were, no matter which country they left to pursue the American Dream?

This land is not just my land. This land is not just your land. This land is *our* land.

APPENDIX
COMING TO—AND STAYING IN—THE UNITED STATES

People from around the world come to the United States for many different reasons. Each person needs a passport that proves he or she is a resident of the home country. (Similarly, every American needs a passport to go to another country.)

People from many countries (there are several exceptions, including Canada) who plan to visit the United States but not live here need a nonimmigrant visa from the U.S. government. They apply through the American embassy in their home countries. Nonimmigrant visas include those given to tourists on vacation, people visiting families and friends in the United States, and people who come for medical treatment.

People who come for business or to attend professional or scientific conferences can get business visas.

If people are staying for more than a short visit—but not permanently—they can get special visas if they are studying at American schools, working for American businesses, coming back and forth as workers on ships or airplanes, or working as foreign journalists covering American news.

Other visas are given to people who want to immigrate to the United States and live here permanently. They need American sponsors who will support their applications. Sponsors can be family members or businesses that will give them jobs for long periods of time. Children from other countries who are adopted by Americans also need visas.

Long-term visas may also be given to refugees, people who have helped America in wartime (for example, translators), and religious workers.

An immigrant with a long-term visa who wants to stay in the United States permanently needs a green card. It is easier for some people to get green cards than others. One has a better chance if he or she has a family member (including a parent, child, sibling, or spouse) who is a citizen of the United States. Chances are also better if one has a permanent job, particularly one that requires special skills. Green cards are also granted to people who invest at least a half-million dollars in American businesses or properties. There is also a green card lottery for immigrants who come from a country that does not have a lot of immigrants to the United States, including Indonesia, Egypt, Russia, Ethiopia, Liberia, and Nepal. (The countries that are included can change every year.) The lottery grants 50,000 green cards a year.

A person with a green card can live in the United States permanently. He or she does not have to become an American citizen, but many do so. The process of becoming a citizen is called "naturalization." There are different requirements for different categories of people. Most should have lived here for at least three (and sometimes five) years. They have to pass a test in the English language about American history and citizenship. As American citizens, they then have all the rights that Americans born here do, including the right to vote.

SELECTED TIME LINE
OF IMMIGRATION HISTORY

1565 The Spanish establish a settlement at St. Augustine, Florida. It is the oldest city founded by Europeans that has been continuously occupied on the mainland of the United States.

1607 Immigrants from England start a permanent colony at Jamestown, Virginia.

1620 The Pilgrims, fleeing religious persecution, settle in Plymouth, Massachusetts.

1776 The original thirteen colonies declare independence from England.

1783 The United States signs a peace treaty with England, ending the American Revolution.

1789 The United States adopts its Constitution, giving Congress power to establish rules for citizenship.

Congress passes a customs act to raise money by calling for a tax on imported goods. Customs inspectors will be set up at major ports, including New York and Boston.

1790 The Naturalization Act declares that "free white person[s]" of "good character" who have been in the United States for two years can become citizens.

1795 The time for residence before an immigrant can become a citizen is extended to five years.

1820–30 A little more than 150,000 immigrants come to the Unites States.

1831–40 Nearly 600,000 immigrants come to the United States.

1845–49 A potato famine leads to mass emigration from Ireland.

1848 The Mexican-American War ends. The United States offers citizenship to Mexicans living in California and the Southwest.

1849 The California Gold Rush draws many immigrants to the Unites States, including Chinese. Those who arrive by ship from foreign countries pass through customs inspections, but there are no limits on immigration.

1841–50 About 1,700,000 immigrants arrive.

1854 The anti-immigrant Native American Party, called "the Know Nothing Party," is formed.

1855 Castle Garden opens to process immigrants entering through New York. It closes in 1890.

1851–60 Nearly 2,600,000 immigrants come to the United States.

1868 The Fourteenth Amendment to the Constitution declares all people born or naturalized in the United States to be citizens.

1861–70 About 2,300,000 immigrants come to the United States. Fewer immigrants come during the American Civil War (1861–65).

1871 Regions of Italy are unified into one country; mass immigration to America begins.

1875 Congress passes an act banning the immigration of Chinese workers being brought to this country without their consent.

1871–80 About 2,800,000 immigrants come to the United States.

1881 Many Jewish immigrants flee to the United States after pogroms in Russia and eastern Europe.

1882 Congress passes the Chinese Exclusion Act, banning Chinese workers from coming to the United States for ten years.

A new Immigration Act requires a 50-cent head tax from each entering immigrant and bans some categories of people, such as those who have no money or are mentally ill.

1886 The Statue of Liberty in New York Harbor is dedicated.

1881–90 About 5,200,000 immigrants enter the United States.

1891 Congress passes an act that creates a national Office of the Superintendent of Immigration (renamed the Bureau of Immigration in 1895). In addition to poor people and those with mental illnesses, the act bans people convicted of crimes and those with contagious diseases.

1892 Ellis Island in New York Harbor opens as the first national immigration processing center. It closes in 1954.

1894 The Immigration Restriction League is formed to oppose mass immigration from southern and eastern Europe.

1891–1900 Nearly 3,700,000 immigrants enter the United States.

1903 Congress passes an act to keep anarchists from entering the United States.

1906 The Bureau of Immigration becomes the Bureau of Immigration and Naturalization

1907 The Gentlemen's Agreement goes into effect with Japan, limiting Japanese immigration.

Congress passes an act saying that women who marry non-American citizens must give up their American citizenship. In 1922, the law is changed to cover only women who marry Asians. The law is not completely repealed until 1940.

1901–10 About 8,800,000 immigrants enter the United States.

1910 The Angel Island inspection station opens in San Francisco Bay to process Asian and Pacific Coast immigrants before they can enter the United States.

1912 Congress passes an act that calls for inspection of agricultural products brought by people from other countries.

1913 California passes a law that prevents any immigrant who cannot become a citizen (mainly Asians) from owning property.

1914 World War I begins in Europe. Immigration declines. The war, which the United States joins in 1917, ends in 1918.

1917 People from Puerto Rico, which became a U.S. territory, have American citizen status.

Congress passes an act that requires a literacy test for all immigrants; the act bans immigration from the "Asian Pacific Triangle" of South Asia, Southeast Asia, and the Pacific Islands (except for American possessions the Philippines and Guam). This is called "the Asiatic barred zone."

1911–20 Some 5,700,000 immigrants enter the United States.

1921 Congress passes an act establishing quotas for European immigrants, based on 3 percent of immigrants from each country who were living in the United States in 1910.

1922 The quota system is extended until 1924.

The Supreme Court upholds the laws denying citizenship to anyone but black and white people in *Ozawa v. United States*.

1923 In *United States v. Bhagat Singh Thind*, the Supreme Court denies citizenship to an Indian who has lived in the United States since 1913 and served in the U.S. army because he is Asian.

1924 Congress passes an act limiting European immigration to 150,000 people per year and setting a quota by country based on 2 percent of the number of immigrants from each country living in the United States in 1890.

The Border Patrol is established.

1929 The U.S. government establishes the rules for deciding quota numbers. Each country's quota is based on the number of immigrants from that country living here in 1890.

1921–30 A little more than 4,100,000 immigrants enter the United States.

1929 The Great Depression begins. Immigration slows. The number of people leaving the United States is more than the number entering each year from 1932 to 1936. Only about 528,000 immigrants enter the country between 1931 and 1940.

1933 With the Nazi government in power, refugees, most of them Jewish, begin to emigrate from Germany.

1934 Congress passes an act giving the Philippines self-government (but not independence). The annual quota for Filipino immigrants is set at 50 people.

1939 World War II begins in Europe and Asia. Emigration from these continents decreases.

1940 Congress passes an act that calls for registering and fingerprinting all noncitizens living in the United States (Alien Registration Act).

The Angel Island immigration station closes.

1941 Japan bombs Pearl Harbor in Hawaii, an American territory. The United States enters World War II.

1942 Executive Order 9066 requires Japanese immigrants and Japanese American citizens living on the West Coast to be interned in camps. In Hawaii, where the Japanese population is large and needed for labor, relatively few are interned.

The United States and Mexico begin the Bracero Program, which allows Mexican workers to come to the United States for limited periods of time. The program ends in 1964.

1943 Congress repeals the 1882 Chinese Exclusion Act. Chinese immigrants become eligible for citizenship.

1945 World War II ends.

1946 Congress passes an act that allows Filipino and Indian immigrants to become citizens. The immigration quotas for each group are very small.

1948 The Displaced Persons Act allows refugees from World War II to enter the United States outside the country quotas. The act is extended in 1950 and lasts until 1952. A little more than 400,000 refugees enter.

1941-50 A little more than 1,000,000 immigrants enter the United States.

1952 The Immigration and Nationality Act (the McCarran-Walter Act) keeps the quota system based on country of origin. The act also allows all Asian immigrants the right to become citizens.

1954 Operation Wetback deports tens of thousands of illegal immigrants living in the Southwest back to Mexico.

1959 After Cuba is taken over by a communist government, refugees begin to flee to the United States.

1951-60 About 2,500,000 immigrants enter the United States.

1965 The Immigration and Nationality Act (the Hart-Celler Act) eliminates national quotas. Instead, the act places quotas on people coming from the Western and Eastern Hemispheres. This is the first quota that applies to immigrants from the Americas.

1966 The Cuban Adjustment Act allows Cuban immigrants in the United States for more than two years to apply for permanent residence, even if they came illegally.

1961-70 About 3,300,000 immigrants enter the United States.

1975 As the Vietnam War ends, refugees from Vietnam and other Southeast Asian countries begin to immigrate to the United States.

1971-80 Nearly 4,500,000 immigrants enter the United States.

1980 The Refugee Act sets a worldwide limit of 270,000 immigrants per year and adds 50,000 slots for refugees. More than 50,000 refugees are usually admitted each year.

1986 The Immigration Reform and Control Act leads to amnesty for nearly 3 million illegal immigrants living in the United States.

1981-90 More than 7,300,000 legal immigrants enter the United States.

1990 Congress raises the worldwide limit on immigrants per year to 700,000.

1991-2000 A little more than 9,000,000 legal immigrants enter the United States.

1994 California voters pass Proposition 187, denying social service benefits and public education for illegal immigrants.

After court challenges, the state restores benefits in 1999.

1996 The Illegal Immigration Reform and Immigrant Responsibility Act increases the number of crimes a legal immigrant can be deported for and expands the Border Patrol.

Congress passes an act cutting social services to legal permanent residents who came to the United States after August 1996.

1997 Congress passes a law that allows Nicaraguans and Cubans to apply for permanent residence and permits other Central Americans and eastern European undocumented immigrants to ask to stop deportation proceedings.

1998 Congress passes a law allowing Haitians to apply for permanent residence.

2001 The fundamentalist Islamic terrorist group Al-Qaeda destroys the World Trade Center in New York and part of the Pentagon in Washington, D.C.

2003 The Immigration and Naturalization Service is put under the new Department of Homeland Security and is responsible for border control, immigration law enforcement, and immigration and citizenship services.

2005 The REAL ID Act increases restrictions on those seeking refugee status and increases immigration enforcement.

2006 The Secure Fence Act calls for 700 miles of fencing along the U.S.-Mexico border.

2010 Arizona passes law SB 1070, requiring immigrants to carry papers, denying illegal immigrants work, allowing police to arrest them without a warrant, and allowing police to check a person's immigrant status for reasonable cause.

2012 The Supreme Court strikes down the first three provisions of SB 1070 but upholds allowing police to check immigrant status.

President Barack Obama begins the Deferred Action for Childhood Arrivals program to stop deportation of young illegal immigrants brought to the United States by their parents when they were children.

2013 By the end of the year, fifteen states have passed Dream Acts supporting young people brought illegally to the United States by their parents. No national Dream Act had passed Congress by 2015.

2013–14 Tens of thousands of Central American children cross the U.S.-Mexico border, sent without documents by their parents because of extreme violence in their home countries.

2014 President Barack Obama declares that about 400,000 undocumented immigrants—parents of U.S. citizens and young people brought by their parents—may remain in the United States.

NOTES

Full bibliographic information for books indicated in the Notes will be found in the Selected Bibliography.

INTRODUCTION

PAGE 3: "Give me . . . golden door!" Poem by Emma Lazarus, "The New Colossus," at www. statueofliberty.org/Statue_of_Liberty.html (accessed July 18, 2014).

PAGE 4: "It lyes . . . the Great." William Byrd II, quoted in Mae M. Ngai and Jon Gjerde, eds., *Major Problems*, p. 48.

PAGE 4: "Any man . . . ever will." Margaret McCarthy, quoted in Roger Daniels, *Coming to America*, p. 130.

PAGE 4: "We came . . . We're satisfied." Albertina di Grazia, quoted in Joan Morrison and Charlotte Fox Zabusky, eds., *American Mosaic*, p. 32.

PAGE 5: "I have no intention . . . opposed to it altogether." George Washington, quoted in Otis L. Graham, *Unguarded Gates*, p. 4.

PAGE 5: "[With] respect to . . . encouragement." George Washington, quoted in ibid.

PAGE 6: "Why should the . . . our Complexion." Benjamin Franklin, quoted in Daniels, *Coming to America*, pp. 109–10.

PAGE 7: The complete lyrics to "This Land Is Your Land" can be found at www.woodyguthrie.org/Lyrics/This_Land.htm (accessed March 7, 2014).

CHAPTER 1
THE BEGINNINGS

PAGE 9: "What then . . . in the world." J. Hector St. John de Crevecoeur, quoted in Daniels, *Coming to America*, pp. 101–2.

PAGE 9: "America is . . . re-forming!" Israel Zangwill, http://www.pluralism.org/encounter/history/melting-pot (accessed February 8, 2015).

PAGE 9: "that the Number . . . Face of the Earth." Benjamin Franklin, quoted in Daniels, *Coming to America*, p. 110.

PAGE 10: On the number of German immigrants. Ilan Stavins, ed., *Becoming Americans*, p. 23.

PAGE 11: Percentage of German and Irish immigrants. Ngai and Gjerde, eds., *Major Problems*, p. 103.

PAGE 11: On voting rights for noncitizens in Midwestern states. Alexander Keyssar, *The Right to Vote*, pp. 32–33.

PAGE 11: "it is most dreadful . . . famine this year." Letter from Hannah Curtis quoted at www.hsp.org/sites/default/files/attachments/curtis_letter_november_24_1845_1.jpg (accessed February 17, 2014).

PAGE 12: "On Sunday . . . ninety-six hours." April 2, 1852, *New York Times* article, http://query.nytimes.com/mem/archive-free/pdf?res=9A05E7D91738E334B-C4A53DFB2668389649FDE (accessed February 15, 2015).

PAGE 12: "huddled together . . . reign supreme." Boston public health report quoted at www.historyplace.com/worldhistory/famine/america.htm (accessed February 17, 2014).

PAGE 13: "I am exceedingly . . . bacon of them." Letter to the *London Times* quoted at www.ushistory.org/us/25f.asp (accessed February 17, 2014).

PAGE 13: "It is a fact . . . of the American people." Samuel F. B. Morse, quoted in Ngai and Gjerde, eds., *Major Problems*, pp. 119–20.

PAGE 14: "On this day . . . idea of Germany is." William Seyffardt, quoted in Thomas Dublin, ed., *Immigrant Voices*, pp. 90, 94, 103.

PAGE 15: "Only those . . . can do well." Anna Maria Schano, quoted in Ngai and Gjerde, eds., *Major Problems*, pp. 105–6.

PAGE 17: "the alternative . . . children." Article reprinted from the *Boston Journal* in the *New York Times*, December 15, 1901, at http://query.nytimes.com/mem/archive-fpee/pdf?res=9F0DE2D-

A173BE733A25756C1A9649D-946097D6CF (accessed July 14, 2014).

PAGE 17: "he became . . . to leave school." Ibid.

PAGE 17: On the Haymarket Riots. John Higham, *Strangers in the Land*, p. 54.

PAGE 18: "long-haired . . . their lives." Ibid., p. 55.

PAGE 18: "Europe's human . . . reptiles." Ibid.

PAGE 18: "There is . . . anarchist." Ibid.

PAGE 18: "The color . . . Anglo-Saxon." Ibid., p. 168.

PAGE 18: "No one . . . certain races." Ibid., p. 101.

CHAPTER 2
THE OTHER EUROPE ARRIVES

PAGE 19: "The day came . . . my baby." Rosa Cassettari told her story to Marie Hall Ets. Ets gave Rosa the last name "Cavalleri" to hide her identity. I have used her real name. Excerpts are from Marie Hall Ets, *Rosa*, p. 162.

PAGE 20: "*America! . . . own land.*" Ibid., p. 164.

PAGE 20: "All us poor . . . soup and bread." Ibid., p. 163.

PAGE 21: "The inside was . . . they shouted.'" Ibid., p. 166.

PAGE 22: "and if on such examination . . . permitted to land." Text of 1882 immigration law, at http://library.uwb.edu/guides/usimmigration/22%20stat%20214.pdf (accessed March 3, 2014).

**PAGE 23: "Numerous

complaints . . . own way."** *New York Tribune* article, quoted in Higham, *Strangers*, p. 67.

PAGE 23: "degrade . . . human beings." Ibid., p. 47.

PAGE 23: "so many cattle . . . serfs." Ibid., p. 48.

PAGE 23: "because . . . to Italians." Ets, *Rosa*, p. 219.

PAGE 23: "my poor rooms . . . with a broom." Ibid., p. 220.

PAGE 24: "My husband . . . have to stand it." Sophie Zurowski, quoted in Morrison and Zabusky, eds., *American Mosaic*, p. 53.

PAGE 25: "[When] I'd saved . . . cutting hair." Joseph Baccardo, quoted in ibid., pp. 67–68.

PAGE 25: "to preserve . . . workingmen." Higham, *Strangers*, p. 46.

PAGE 25: Essay prize for "The Evil Effects of Unrestricted Immigration." Ibid., p. 41.

PAGE 26: "also any person . . . others to come." Text of 1891 immigration law, at http://library.uwb.edu/guides/usimmigration/26%20stat%201084.pdf (accessed March 3, 2014).

PAGE 27: "What are they . . . any trouble." John Daroubian, quoted in Morrison and Zabusky, eds., *American Mosaic*, pp. 23–24.

PAGE 28: "so when we . . . to my mother." Faye Lundsky, quoted in Peter Morton Coan, *Toward a Better Life*, p 49.

PAGE 28: "America . . . human hands." Walter Lindstrom, quoted in Morrison and Zabusky, eds., *American Mosaic*, p. 5.

**PAGE 28: "My mother said . . .

on his own." Faye Lundsky, quoted in Coan, *Toward a Better Life*, pp. 49, 50, 52.

PAGE 28: **"We started work . . . did the same thing."** Pauline Newman, quoted in Morrison and Zabusky, eds., *American Mosaic*, p. 10.

PAGE 30: **"I remember . . . chicken soup."** Faye Lundsky, quoted in Coan, *Toward a Better Life*, p. 50.

PAGE 30: **On the justifications for racism**, see Daniels, *Coming to America*, p. 276, and Higham, *Strangers*, Chapter 6.

PAGE 31: **"The hereditary . . . to contend."** Prescott F. Hall, quoted in Higham, *Strangers*, p. 44.

PAGE 31: **"to be peopled . . . and stagnant."** Daniels, *Coming to America*, p. 276.

PAGE 31: **"to smother . . . institutions."** Higham, *Strangers*, p. 79.

PAGE 32: **"The illiteracy test . . . of the United States."** Henry Cabot Lodge, quoted in Higham, *Strangers*, p. 101.

PAGE 32: **"stupendous growth . . . best citizens."** Grover Cleveland, quoted in Daniels, *Coming to America*, p. 277.

PAGE 33: **On 18 percent foreign-born.** Higham, *Strangers*, p. 216.

PAGE 33: **"These handicapped . . . toward them."** Ibid., p. 217

PAGE 33: **"the simple . . . Americans."** Theodore Roosevelt, quoted in ibid., p. 198.

PAGE 33: **"there was . . . Americanka then."** Sonia

Walinsky, quoted in Morrison and Zabusky, eds., *American Mosaic*, p. 1.

PAGE 35: **Text of 1921 Emergency Immigration Act**, at http://library.uwb.edu/guides/usimmigration/42%20stat%205.pdf (accessed March 3, 2014).

PAGE 35: **355,000 a year.** Mae M. Ngai, *Impossible Subjects*, p. 20.

PAGE 35: **9.9 million.** Roger Daniels, *Guarding the Golden Door*, p. 45.

PAGE 35: **On drop in number of immigrants.** Ngai, *Impossible Subjects*, p. 272.

PAGE 35: **"The old Americans . . . of America."** Higham, *Strangers*, p. 264.

PAGE 36: **"Today, instead . . . definitely ended."** Albert Johnson, quoted in Daniels, *Coming to America*, pp. 283–84.

PAGE 37: **Johnson-Reed Act**, at http://library.uwb.edu/guides/usimmigration/43%20stat%20153.pdf (accessed March 3, 2014).

PAGE 37: **All figures from "Immigration Quotas Based on National Origin" table**, in Ngai, *Impossible Subjects*, pp. 28–29.

CHAPTER 3
THE OTHER SHORE

PAGE 38: **"I happened . . . I decided."** Frank Tomori, quoted in Ronald Takaki, *Strangers from a Different Shore*, p. 52.

PAGE 39: **"There were four . . . with the rice."** Ibid., p. 33.

PAGE 39: **On Chinese immigration statistics.** Ibid., p. 31.

PAGE 40: **"[The] concentration . . . education."** Ibid., p. 82.

PAGE 40: **"Certain . . . of feeling."** Ibid., p. 100.

PAGE 41: **Text of Naturalization Act of 1790**, in Franklin Odo, ed., *The Columbia Documentary History*, pp. 13–14.

PAGE 41: **"aliens of . . . African descent."** Stavins, ed., *Becoming Americans*, p. 700.

PAGE 41: **"The 60,000 . . . stronger races."** Henry George, quoted in Daniels, *Guarding the Golden Door*, p. 13.

PAGE 42: **"We respectfully . . . advantage of all."** Odo, ed., *The Columbia Documentary History*, p. 50.

PAGE 43: **"children . . . Chinese descent."** California Political Code, at https://books.google.com/books?id=KNA3AAAA-IAAJ&pg=PA389&lp-g=PA389&dq=%22for+chil-dren+of+Mongolian+or+Chi-nese+descent%22+1885&-source=bl&ots=D4jtlvZm-he&sig=ErQKoduWzLjP8jI2-57Ra1ErtBiY&hl=en&sa=X&ei=G-2DiVLWUKLeOsQT1nYCwB-g&ved=0CCUQ6AEwAQ#v=one-page&q=%22for%20children%20of%20Mongolian%20or%20Chinese%20descent%22%201885&f=false (accessed February 16, 2015).

PAGE 44: **Text of 1882 Chinese Exclusion Act**, at www.mtholy-oke.edu/acad/intrel/chinex.htm (accessed May 16, 2014).

PAGE 44: **On first border patrols.** Ngai, *Impossible Subjects*, p. 64.

PAGE 45: "not much bigger . . . all kinds." Robert Eric Barde, *Immigration at the Golden Gate*, p. 62.

PAGE 45: "'There are . . . in their papers." Ibid., p. 70.

PAGE 45: "'Here you are . . . you care?'" Wong Hock Won, quoted in ibid.

PAGE 46: On the number of immigrants who passed through Angel Island, at www.sfgate.com/bayarea/article/Upgraded-Angel-Island-museum-reopens-Sunday-3171731.php (accessed November 7, 2014).

PAGE 46: On comparing Angel and Ellis Islands, ibid.

PAGE 46: On "paper sons and daughters," at www.angelisland.org/history/united-states-immigration-station-usis (accessed November 7, 2014).

PAGE 47: "I used to . . . my mind." Takaki, *Strangers*, pp. 8–9.

PAGE 47: "What strikes me . . . and grass." Ibid., p. 43.

PAGE 47: "Huge . . . ocean." Ibid., p. 41.

PAGE 48: "menace . . . labor." Henry Gage, quoted in ibid., p. 201.

PAGE 48: "went through . . . North America." Chiura Obata, quoted in Odo, ed., *The Columbia Documentary History*, p. 138.

PAGE 49: "Would you . . . public schools." Takaki, *Strangers*, p. 201.

PAGE 49: "all . . . Oriental Public School." Ibid.

PAGE 50: "The persecutions . . . several times." Ibid.

PAGE 50: "aliens . . . citizenship." Ibid., p. 203.

PAGE 51: "Our mission . . . their arrival." Koyu Uchida, quoted in Odo, ed., *The Columbia Documentary History*, pp. 172–73.

PAGE 52: "Ninang . . . keep us." Angeles Monrayo, *Tomorrow's Memories*, pp. 186, 191.

PAGE 52: On Stockton, California. Ibid., p. 264.

PAGE 52: "camp . . . outhouses." Mary Paik Lee, quoted in Dublin, ed., *Immigrant Voices*, p. 177.

PAGE 52: "first day . . . blow on the neck." Ibid., pp. 180–81.

PAGE 53: "first experience . . . to America." Ibid., p. 183.

PAGE 53: "When we . . . the subject." Ibid., p. 201.

PAGE 53: "I studied . . . in the head." Younghill Kang, quoted in Odo, ed., *The Columbia Documentary History*, p. 215.

PAGE 53: "Do you wonder . . . and opportunity." Takaki, *Strangers*, pp. 63–64.

PAGE 54: 6,400 immigrants. Ibid., p. 294.

PAGE 54: "The civic . . . new stream." Ibid., p. 297.

PAGE 54: Text of 1917 Immigration Act, at http://library.uwb.edu/guides/usimmigration/39%20stat%20874.pdf (accessed July 18, 2014).

PAGE 55: Figures on numbers and percentage of Asians in Hawaii. Takaki, *Strangers*, p. 132.

PAGE 55: "We worked . . . constantly" and "would gallop . . . whip." Ibid., p. 135.

PAGE 56: "to the Control . . . #10710." Monica Sone, quoted in ibid., p. 393.

PAGE 57: "No houses . . . baked earth." Ibid., p. 395.

CHAPTER 4
SOUTH OF OUR BORDER

PAGE 59: "Some Americans . . . ask of life?" Paola, Vanessa, and Sara Garcia, quoted in Pamela Constable and Scott Clement, "Hispanics often lead the way in their faith in the American Dream, poll finds," at www.washingtonpost.com/local/hispanics-often-lead-the-way-in-their-faith-in-the-american-dream-poll-finds/2014/01/30/c9d4d498-6c2a-11e3-b405-7e360f7e9fd2_story.html (accessed February 16, 2015).

PAGE 59: On poll. Ibid.

PAGE 60: 80,000 Mexicans. Daniels, *Coming to America*, p. 307.

PAGE 60: On Mexicans in Southwest becoming Americans. Ngai, *Impossible Subjects*, pp. 50–52.

PAGE 60: 700,000 Mexicans. Dublin, ed., *Immigrant Voices*, p. 203.

PAGE 61: On border control history, at www.cbp.gov/border-security/along-us-borders/history (accessed November 10, 2014).

PAGE 61: On U.S.-Mexico border crossings in 2014, at www.immigrationpolicy.org/just-facts/lost-shadow-fence

(accessed November 7, 2014).

PAGE 61: "Lower Sacramento . . . stables." Ernesto Galarza, quoted in Dublin, ed., *Immigrant Voices*, p. 218.

PAGE 62: "The *colonia* . . . could live." Ibid., p. 220.

PAGE 64: "The total . . . very quickly." Manuel Gamio, *Mexican Immigration to the United States*, p. 204.

PAGE 64: "They . . . your groceries." Valente Ramírez, quoted in Ricardo Romo, "Responses to Mexican Immigration, 1910–1930," in Michael R. Ornelas, ed., *Beyond 1848*, p. 119.

PAGE 64: On Ramón Lizárraga. Ibid., p. 118.

PAGE 65: "in poor condition . . . cots." Aureliano Ocampo, quoted in Ngai, *Impossible Subjects*, p. 141.

PAGE 65: "As a wetback . . . like a man." Carlos Morales, quoted in ibid., p. 146.

PAGE 67: "The next time . . . the burro." José Garcia, quoted in Morrison and Zabusky, eds., *American Mosaic*, p. 351.

PAGE 67: "alarming . . . the border." Joseph M. Swing, quoted in Ngai, *Impossible Subjects*, p. 155.

PAGE 68: "Their home life . . . or employment." Ibid., p. 160.

PAGE 68: "needed a . . . to leave." Tomás Rivera, . . . *And the Earth Did Not Devour Him*, p. 103.

PAGE 68: "was trying . . . was my house." Cesar Millan, quoted in Coan, *Toward a Better Life*, pp. 282–83.

PAGE 69: "Mexico is . . . come true." Ibid., p. 280.

PAGE 69: "I am rising . . . will be true." Jaime Alvarez, quoted in Morrison and Zabusky, eds., *American Mosaic*, p. 358.

PAGE 69: "the weather . . . of the people." Piri Thomas, quoted in Dublin, ed., *Immigrant Voices*, pp. 261, 263.

PAGE 70: "My mouth . . . in New York." Aurora Flores, at www.pbs.org/latino-americans/en/blog/2013/09/03/Boricua-Christmas-New-York/ (accessed February 16, 2015).

CHAPTER 5
SEEKING SAFETY AND LIBERTY

PAGE 71: "I decided . . . expression." Alejandro, quoted in Ngai and Gjerde, eds., *Major Problems*, pp. 529–30.

PAGE 72: "lowered [a] boat . . . Coca-Cola." Ibid.

PAGE 72: "because of persecution . . . opinion." Ibid., p. 526.

PAGE 73: "our plans . . . creed." Myron Taylor, quoted in Daniels, *Guarding the Golden Door*, p. 77.

PAGE 73: "pushed us aside . . . the house." Elise Radell, quoted in Morrison and Zabusky, eds., *American Mosaic*, p. 138.

PAGE 74: "You couldn't . . . a week." Ibid., p. 141.

PAGE 76: On the 1948 Displaced Persons Act. Daniels, *Guarding the Golden Door*, p. 109 and http://library.uwb.edu/guides/USimmigration/1948_displaced_persons_act.html (accessed November 10, 2014).

PAGE 77: "For me . . . my country now." Aniela Szeliga, quoted in Coan, *Toward a Better Life*, p. 158.

PAGE 77: "I was in my . . . on the airplane." Ava Rado-Harte, quoted in ibid., pp. 166, 167, 170.

PAGE 78: "declare[d] . . . upheld." Lyndon Johnson, quoted in ibid., p. 198.

PAGE 79: "To me . . . have an opinion." Emilio Estefan, quoted in ibid., p. 224.

PAGE 79: "On April 28 . . . the children." Trong Nguyen, quoted in Dublin, ed., *Immigrant Voices*, pp. 278.

PAGE 80: "Vietnam is . . . back home." Thanh Nguyen, quoted in ibid.

PAGE 80: "more than fifty . . . McDonald's." Trong Nguyen, quoted in ibid., p. 289.

PAGE 81: "We didn't know . . . a better life." Tuan Nguyen, quoted at www.vietka.com/Vietnamese_Boat_People/Road_to_US.htm (accessed June 15, 2014).

PAGE 82: "They came . . . are *very* cool!" Roya, quoted in Judith M. Blohn and Terri Lapinsky, *Kids Like Me*, pp. 142, 144.

PAGE 83: "131,000 refugees." www.nytimes.com/2007/04/29/us/29youth.html?pagewanted=all&_r=0 (accessed February 16, 2015).

PAGE 83: "20,000 refugees." www.nytimes.com/1999/04/07/world/crisis-balkans-haven-us-chooses-guantanamo-bay-base-cuba-for-refugee-site.html (accessed February 16, 2015).

PAGE 83: "In 1998 . . . was shot." Fatim, quoted in Blohn and

Lapinsky, *Kids Like Me*, pp. 133–34.

PAGE 83: "If we get . . . housing market" and Gallup Poll results. Nhi T. Lieu, *The American Dream in Vietnamese*, p. 10.

PAGE 83: "There will . . . for soccer." Lee Swaney, quoted in Ngai and Gjerde, eds., *Major Problems*, p. 534.

PAGE 83: "Refugees . . . chance on them." John Kerry, at www.huffingtonpost.com/john-kerry/the-refugee-act-more-reas_b_499575.html (accessed August 16, 2014).

PAGE 84: "By protecting . . . traditions." Ted Kennedy, at www.fromthesquare.org/?p=672 (accessed August 16, 2014).

PAGE 84: "I was in jail . . . human rights." Carmen, at www.nwo.media.xs2.net/articles/84_05sal-vadoran.html (accessed June 14, 2014).

PAGE 84: On Haitian immigrant statistics. www.oas.org/juridico/english/gavigane.html (accessed June 14, 2014).

PAGE 85: "I did not know . . . days and days." Clemantine Wamariya, at www.yaledailynews.com/blog/2010/09/09/rwandan-refugee-reaches-out (accessed June 27, 2014).

PAGE 86: 122 North Koreans, at www.38north.org/2011/09/rcohen092011 (accessed June 17, 2014).

PAGE 86: "I had to do . . . with friends." Joseph Kim, at www.layouth.com/interview-with-a-north-korean-refugee (accessed June 27, 2014).

PAGE 86: "I did not . . . act of

love." Joseph Kim, at www.washingtonpost.com/blogs/worldviews/wp/2013/06/21/hope-brought-me-to-america-a-north-korean-defector-tells-his-inspiring-story (accessed June 27, 2014).

PAGE 86: On Iraqi immigrant statistics. https://refugeeresettlementwatch.wordpress.com/2014/09/13/how-many-iraqi-refugees-came-to-america-since-911-how-are-they-doing/ (accessed February 16, 2015).

PAGE 86: "I never thought . . . my family." Adil Ibrahim, at http://america.aljazeera.com/articles/2013/8/20/reborn-in-the-u-sa.html (accessed July 9, 2014).

PAGE 87: 55,000 Afghan refugees, 2,300 Afghan refugees, at http://data.un.org/Data.aspx?d=UNHCR&f=indID%3A-Type-Ref (accessed July 10, 2014).

PAGE 87: On number of Syrian refugees, at www.reuters.com/article/2014/02/05/us-syria-crisis-usa-refugees-idUS-BREA141ZQ20140205 (accessed July 10, 2014).

PAGE 88: "There are . . . having parents." Clemantine Wamariya, at http://yaledailynews.com/blog/2010/09/09/rwandan-refugee-reaches out (accessed July 10, 2014).

PAGE 88: "Welcoming and accepting . . . promote it." Wamariya, at www.huffingtonpost.com/clemantine-wamariya/why-refugees-are-natural-leaders-of-the-third-met-

ric_b_3742478.html (accessed July 10, 2014).

CHAPTER 6
THIS LAND IS WHOSE LAND?

PAGE 89: "I didn't want . . . has overcome." Perla Rabor Rigor, quoted in Ngai and Gjerde, eds., *Major Problems*, pp. 493, 494–95.

PAGE 90: "I believe . . . the strain." Patrick McCarran, quoted at www.upa.pdx.edu/IMS/currentprojects/TAHv3/Content/PDFs/Immigration_Act_1952.pdf (accessed June 28, 2014).

PAGE 90: "The basis . . . citizenry." Harry Truman, quoted in Daniels, *Guarding the Golden Door*, p. 121.

PAGE 91: Text of McCarran-Walter Act, at http://library.uwb.edu/guides/usimmigration/66%20stat%20163.pdf (accessed July 18, 2014).

PAGE 91: "By 1959 . . . totally American." Jacques Pépin, quoted in Coan, *Toward a Better Life*, pp. 186–87, 195.

PAGE 92: On immigration statistics, 1952–65. Daniels, *Guarding the Golden Door*, p. 123.

PAGE 92: "In America . . . society," at www.koreanamericanstory.org/my-korean-american-story-diana-yu (accessed August 17, 2014).

PAGE 92: On increasing numbers of Asians immigrating to the United States. www.pewsocialtrends.org/2012/06/19/the-rise-of-asian-americans (accessed August 17, 2013).

PAGE 93: Text of 1965 Immigration and Nationality Act, at http://library.uwb.edu/guides/usimmigration/79%20stat%20911.pdf (accessed July 18, 2014).

PAGE 94: "will not flood . . . their jobs." Ted Kennedy, quoted at www.cis.org/1965ImmigrationAct-MassImmigration (accessed July 10, 2014).

PAGE 94: "It is obvious . . . their course." Sidney Yates, quoted at ibid.

PAGE 94: On number of legal immigrants. Daniels, *Guarding the Golden Door*, pp. 137, 139.

PAGE 95: On number of illegal immigrants. David A. Gerber, *American Immigration*, p. 125.

PAGE 95: "I was the . . . tolerant." Tunde Ayobami, quoted in Morrison and Zabusky, eds., *American Mosaic* pp. 404, 407–8.

PAGE 95: "I spoke . . . can be both." Dr. E. Murat Tuzcu, quoted in Coan, *Toward a Better Life*, pp. 270–71.

PAGE 96: "During . . . unfortunate." Fr. Theodore Hesburgh, quoted in Daniels, *Guarding the Golden Door*, p. 221.

PAGE 96: Text of 1986 Immigration Reform and Control Act, at http://library.uwb.edu/guides/usimmigration/100%20stat%203359.pdf (accessed July 18, 2014).

PAGE 96: On number of illegal immigrants who became permanent residents. Daniels, *Guarding the Golden Door*, p. 229.

PAGE 96: Text of 1990

Immigration and Nationality Act, at http://library.uwb.edu/guides/usimmigration/1990_immigration_and_nationality_act.html (accessed July 18, 2014).

PAGE 96: "In my culture . . . work for it." Golly Ramnath, quoted in Coan, *Toward a Better Life*, pp. 302–3.

PAGE 97: "I received . . . New Yorkers." Kiril Tarpov, quoted in ibid., pp. 309–10, 311–12.

PAGE 98: "I had been . . . not make it." Carlos Escobar, quoted in ibid., pp. 295, 297.

PAGE 99: "This was . . . life." Ibid., p.298.

PAGE 99: On nationalities of illegal immigrants, at www.pewhispanic.org/2011/02/01/ii-current-estimates-and-trends (accessed July 11, 2014).

PAGE 100: On illegal immigrants crossing from Canada. http://cnsnews.com/news/article/canadian-border-bigger-terror-threat-mexican-border-says-border-patrol-chief and www.usimmigration.com/illegal-immigrants-through-canada.html (both accessed July 11, 2014).

PAGE 100: On illegal immigrants paying taxes, at www.immigration.procon.org/view.answers.php?questionID=000789 (accessed August 16, 2014).

PAGE 100: "We support . . . citizens." Republican platform, quoted in Daniels, *Guarding the Golden Door*, p. 245.

PAGE 100: On 1996 law restricting benefits, at www.nilc.org/over-

view-immeligfedprograms.html (accessed July 11, 2014).

PAGE 101: On Supreme Court decision, Arizona SB 1070, at www.cnn.com/interactive/2012/06/us/scotus.immigration/?pos=canon (accessed July 11, 2014).

PAGE 101: "[my] uncle . . . immigration laws." www.weareamericastories.org/2012/02/how-our-backwards-immigration-system-tore-our-family-apart (accessed July 11, 2014).

PAGE 102: "Unfortunately, my little . . . graduation." Antonio Alarcón, quoted at www.fwd.us/antonio_story (accessed July 11, 2014).

PAGE 103: "I am not . . . proven ourselves." Pierre Berastaín, quoted at www.durbin.senate.gov/public/index.cfm/hot-topics?ContentRecord_id=d17ca59b-7420-441b-9ac2-2faf7549e9d0 (accessed February 16, 2015).

PAGE 103: "I would . . . deport them." Manny Bartsch, quoted at ibid.

PAGE 104: "My family . . . bright future." Al Okere, quoted at ibid.

PAGE 104: Provisions of DACA, at www.whitehouse.gov/blog/2012/08/15/deferred-action-childhood-arrivals-who-can-be-considered (accessed July 18, 2014).

PAGE 105: On children crossing from Central America, at www.theguardian.com/world/2014/jul/09/central-america-child-migrants-us-border-crisis (accessed July 18, 2014).

PAGE 105: "The first thing . . . leave." www.nytimes.com/2014/07/10/world/americas/fleeing-gangs-children-head-to-us-border.html (accessed July 18, 2014).

PAGE 105: "It's a serious . . . gang." Ibid.

PAGE 105: On Obama's executive act allowing some illegal immigrants to stay, in David Nakamura, "Obama Acts to Overhaul Immigration," *Washington Post*, November 21, 2014, pp. 1, 8.

SELECTED BIBLIOGRAPHY

*Indicates a book suitable for children

Barde, Robert Eric. *Immigration at the Golden Gate: Passenger Ships, Exclusion, and Angel Island*. Westport, Conn.: Praeger, 2008.

* Bausum, Ann. *Denied, Detained, Deported: Stories from the Dark Side of American Immigration*. Washington, D.C.: National Geographic, 2009.

* Behnke, Alison. *Mexicans in America*. Minneapolis: Lerner Publications, 2005.

* Blohn, Judith M., and Terri Lapinsky. *Kids Like Me: Voices of the Immigrant Experience*. Boston: Intercultural Press, 2006.

Coan, Peter Morton. *Toward a Better Life: America's New Immigrants in Their Own Words from Ellis Island to the Present*. Amherst, N.Y.: Prometheus Books, 2011.

Daniels, Roger. *Coming to America: A History of Immigration and Ethnicity in American Life*. 2nd ed. New York: Harper Perennial, 2002.

Daniels, Roger. *Guarding the Golden Door: American Immigration Policy and Immigrants Since 1882*. New York: Hill and Wang, 2004.

Dublin, Thomas, ed. *Immigrant Voices: New Lives in America, 1773–1986*. Urbana, Ill.: University of Illinois Press, 1993.

Ets, Marie Hall. *Rosa: The Life of an Italian Immigrant*. 2nd ed. Madison, Wis.: University of Wisconsin Press, 1999.

Gamio, Manuel. *Mexican Immigration to the United States: A Study of Human Migration and Adjustment*. Chicago: University of Chicago Press: 1930.

Gerber, David A. *American Immigration: A Very Short Introduction*. New York: Oxford University Press, 2011.

Graham, Otis L. *Unguarded Gates: A History of America's Immigration Crisis*. Lanham, Md.: Rowman & Littlefield, 2004.

Handlin, Oscar. *The Uprooted: The Epic Story of the Great Migration That Made the American People*. 2nd ed. Boston: Little, Brown, 1979.

Higham, John. *Strangers in the Land: Patterns of American Nativism 1860–1925*. 2nd ed. New Brunswick, N.J.: Rutgers University Press, 2001.

Hoerder, Dirk, and Leslie Page Moch, eds. *European Migrants: Global and Local Perspectives*. Boston: Northeastern University Press, 1996.

* Hoobler, Dorothy and Thomas. *We Are Americans: Voices of the Immigrant Experience*. New York: Scholastic, 2003.

Hutner, Gordon, ed. *Immigrant Voices: Twenty-four Narratives on Becoming an American*. New York: Signet, 1999.

* Jango-Cohen, Judith. *Ellis Island*. New York: Children's Press, 2005.

Keyssar, Alexander. *The Right to Vote: The Contested History of Democracy in the United States*. New York: Basic Books, 2000.

Lawlor, Veronica. *I Was Dreaming to Come to America: Memories from the Ellis Island Oral History Project*. New York: Viking, 1995.

* Levine, Ellen. *If Your Name Was Changed at Ellis Island*. New York: Scholastic, 1993.

Lieu, Nhi T. *The American Dream in Vietnamese*. Minneapolis:

University of Minnesota Press, 2011.

Monrayo, Angeles. *Tomorrow's Memories: A Diary, 1924–1928.* Rizaline R. Raymundo, ed. Honolulu: University of Hawai'i Press, 2003.

Morrison, Joan, and Charlotte Fox Zabusky, eds. *American Mosaic: The Immigrant Experience in the Words of Those Who Lived It.* Pittsburgh: University of Pittsburgh Press, 1993

Ngai, Mae M. *Impossible Subjects: Illegal Aliens and the Making of Modern America.* Princeton, N.J.: Princeton University Press, 2004.

Ngai, Mae M., and Jon Gjerde, eds. *Major Problems in American Immigration History: Documents and Essays.* 2nd ed. Boston: Wadsworth, Cengage Learning, 2013.

Odo, Franklin, ed. *The Columbia Documentary History of the Asian American Experience.* New York: Columbia University Press, 2002.

Ornelas, Michael R., ed. *Beyond 1848: Readings in the Modern Chicano Historical Experience.* Dubuque, Iowa: Kendall/Hunt, 1993.

Osborne, Linda Barrett, and Paolo Battaglia. *Explorers Emigrants Citizens: A Visual History of the Italian American Experience from the Collections of the Library of Congress.* Modena, Italy: Anniversary Books/Washington, D.C.: Library of Congress, 2013.

* Peacock, Louise. *At Ellis Island: A History in Many Voices.* New York: Atheneum Books for Young Readers, 2007.

* Reef, Catherine. *Ellis Island.*

New York: Maxwell Macmillan International, 1991.

Rivera, Tomás. . . . *And the Earth Did Not Devour Him.* Evangelina Vigil-Pinon, trans. Houston: Arte Publico Press, 1987.

* Smith, David J. *If America Were a Village: A Book About the People of the United States.* Toronto, Canada: Kids Can Press, 2009.

Stavins, Ilan, ed. *Becoming Americans: Four Centuries of Immigrant Writing.* New York: Library of America, 2009.

* Stefoff, Rebecca. *A Century of Immigration: 1820–1924.* New York: Marshall Cavendish Benchmark, 2007.

Takaki, Ronald. *Strangers from a Different Shore: A History of Asian Americans.* 2nd ed. Boston: Little, Brown, 1998.

ACKNOWLEDGMENTS

I don't believe there are a better editor and art director in publishing than Howard Reeves and Maria Middleton. I've had the good fortune to work with them for the third time on this book. Howard has the knack of asking simple questions that don't always have simple answers but invariably improve the clarity and depth of the text. He leaves me time to create but is always there when I need him. Maria has a talent for transforming words and illustrations into works of art. Her books are simply beautiful.

I am grateful to editorial assistant Orlando Dos Reis not only for deftly dealing with the mass of drafts and images I've sent him but also for his thoughtful reading of the manuscript. His suggestions led me to expand in new directions, and, as an immigrant himself, his praise for my treatment of the topic meant a lot to me. Thanks, too, to managing editor Jim Armstrong, for directing the complex and intense business of production; and to copyeditor Renée Cafiero and fact-checker David M. Webster, whose insights into history

and attention to detail greatly contributed to accuracy. I also appreciate the work of designer Sara Corbett, who ensured that the overall design concept was carried out on every page.

Grazie mille to Paolo Battaglia, Italian publisher and coauthor with me of *Explorers Emigrants Citizens* (*Trovare l'America* in Italy), a history of Italian Americans. It was Paolo's idea to write the book out of concern for the treatment of immigrants to Italy. I knew little about my great-grandparents and their experience as immigrants here, but I agreed. My research was an eye-opener. I understood that Italian Americans had been discriminated against, but I had not realized the extent of the fear, prejudice, and hatred that had been directed not only against them, but at many other immigrant groups to this country. My work with Paolo led directly to the research and writing of *This Land Is Our Land*.

Finding and acquiring images for a book is a complicated process. Thanks to those who were especially helpful and gracious: Nilda I. Rivera of the Museum of the City of New York; Aimee Hess Nash of the Library of Congress; Dorothy Cordova of the Filipino American National Historical Society; Cyndy Gilley of Do You Graphics; Tia Reber of the Bishop Museum in Hawaii; photographer Jason Redmond; and Patricia Violante, Aurora Flores, and Orlando Dos Reis for providing family photos that add a much-appreciated personal touch.

Special thanks to my husband, Bob, my children, Catherine and Nick, and my daughter-in-law, Mary Kate Hurley. Writing a book takes you into other worlds, but Bob continually took care of me in this one. (At least with him I ate.) Catherine was always there to reassure me and refocus me, and Mary Kate to lend her support. Finally, Nick, a professor of American history, guided me from the very beginning with his suggestions for exemplary sources, his discussion of difficult topics, and his ability to help me write a history for young readers that strides the fine line between being too complicated and being oversimplified. Many writers say, "It wouldn't have been possible without them," and might be exaggerating. But in this case, it's true.

ILLUSTRATION CREDITS

page i: Library of Congress LC-DIG-pga-03455.

page ii (clockwise from top right): AP Photo/*Herald News*, Leslie Barbara; Jacob A. Riis/ Museum of the City of New York; Heather DiMasi/NOWCast SA; Library of Congress LC-G403-T01-0105-B; State Archives of Florida; Library of Congress LC-USW33-031866-C.

page 2: Library of Congress LC-DIG-pga-03455.

page 3: Courtesy of the author.

page 4: Library of Congress LC-USZC4-2968.

page 6: Library of Congress LC-USZ62-45439.

page 7: Library of Congress LC-USZ62-23711.

page 8: Library of Congress LC-USZC4-8079.

page 10: Library of Congress LC-USZ62-100310.

page 12: Library of Congress LC-USZ62-2022.

page 14: Library of Congress LC-USZC4-1216.

page 15: Library of Congress LC-USZ62-19431.

page 16: Library of Congress LC-DIG-ppmsca-31563.

page 17: Library of Congress LC-USZ62-796.

page 19: Library of Congress LC-USZ62-67910.

page 20: Byron Company/Museum of the City of New York.

page 21: Thomas Chambers (1808–1869)/Museum of the City of New York.

page 22: Museum of the City of New York.

page 24: Library of Congress LC-USZC4-2654.

page 25: Museum of the City of New York.

page 26: Library of Congress LC-DIG-ds-03648.

page 27, top: Library of Congress LC-USZ62-7386.

page 27, bottom: Jacob A. Riis/ Museum of the City of New York.

page 28: Library of Congress LC-DIG-nclc-04109.

page 29: Library of Congress LC-DIG-nclc-00823.

page 30: Library of Congress LC-DIG-nclc-00008.

page 31: Library of Congress LC-USZ62-101889.

page 32: Library of Congress LC-USZC4-5845.

page 34: Library of Congress LC-DIG-nclc-04529.

page 35: Library of Congress LC-DIG-nclc-04549.

page 36, top: Byron Company/ Museum of the City of New York.

page 36, bottom: Byron Company/ Museum of the City of New York.

page 38: Library of Congress LC-USZ62-50743.

page 40: Library of Congress LC-G403-T01-0105-B.

page 41: Library of Congress LC-USZ62-53346.

page 42, top: Library of Congress LC-USZC2-1213.

page 42, bottom: Library of Congress LC-USZ62-136179.

page 43: Library of Congress LC-USZ62-103143.

page 44: Courtesy National Archives (photo no. NWDNS-090-G-124-0479).

page 46: Courtesy National Archives (photo no. NWDNS-090-G-124-2038).

page 47: Library of Congress LC-DIG-highsm-25218.

page 48: Courtesy National Archives (photo no. NWDNS-090-G-152-2040.

page 49: Courtesy National Archives (photo no. NWDNS-090-G-152-2038.

page 50: *Los Angeles Times* Photographic Archives (Collection 1429). UCLA Library Special Collections, Charles E. Young Research Library, UCLA.

page 51: Library of Congress LC-USZ6-1185.

page 53: Courtesy of Los Angeles Public Library.

page 54: Courtesy Southern Oregon Historical Society.

page 55: Courtesy Bishop Museum, Honolulu, Hawaii.

page 56, top: Library of Congress LC-USF33-013290-M3.

page 56, bottom: Courtesy National Archives (photo no. NWDNS-210-G-B78).

page 57: Library of Congress LC-DIG-ppprs-00285.

page 58: Library of Congress LC-USZC4-5667.

page 60: Library of Congress LC-USZC4-2957.

page 61: Library of Congress LC-DIG-ggbain-15424.

page 62: Library of Congress maps collection.

page 63, top: Library of Congress LC-DIG-fsa-8b31696.

page 63, bottom: Photograph by Donna Burton. US Customs and Border Protection.

page 64: Library of Congress LC-USW3-031006-D.

page 65: Library of Congress LC-USW33-031866-C.

page 66: Library of Congress LC-DIG-ds-02129.

page 67: Library of Congress LC-USF34-018222-E.

page 70: Courtesy of Aurora Flores.

page 71: State Archives of Florida.

page 73: Library of Congress LC-DIG-ppmsca-05638.

page 74: United Nations Photo.

page 76: United Nations Photo.

page 78: State Archives of Florida.

page 80: Courtesy National Archives (photo no. NWDNS-CFD-DN-SN-84-09740).

page 81: United Nations Photo.

page 82: United Nations Photo.

page 85: United Nations Photo.

page 87: United Nations Photo.

page 88: United Nations Photo.

page 89: Courtesy of Filipino American National Historical Society.

page 92: Courtesy of Patricia Violante.

page 93: Photograph by Yoichi Okamoto. LBJ Presidential Library.

page 94: AP Photo/*Herald News*, Leslie Barbaro.

page 95: Courtesy of Orlando Dos Reis.

page 97: Omar Torres/AFP/ Getty Images.

page 98: Heather DiMasi/ NOWCast SA.

page 100: AP Photo/Gregory Bull.

page 102: AP Photo/Kathy Willens.

page 104: Photograph by Jason Redmond.

page 106: REUTERS/Lucy Nicholson.

INDEX